Engaging God's Word

Genesis

Engage Bible Studies

Tools That Transform

Engage Bible Studies

an imprint of

 COMMUNITY BIBLE STUDY

Engaging God's Word: Genesis
Copyright © 2012, 2014 by Community Bible Study. All rights reserved.
ISBN 978-1-62194-007-4

Published by Community Bible Study
790 Stout Road
Colorado Springs, CO 80921-3802
1-800-826-4181
www.communitybiblestudy.org

Printed in the United States of America.

Contents

Introduction

Welcome to the life-changing adventure of engaging with God's Word! Whether this is the first time you've opened a Bible or you've studied the Scriptures all your life, good things are in store for you. Studying the Bible is unlike any other kind of study you have ever done. That's because the Word of God is *"living and active"* (Hebrews 4:12) and transcends time and cultures. The earth and heavens as we know them will one day pass away, but God's Word never will (Mark 13:31). It's as relevant to your life today as it was to the people who wrote it down centuries ago. And the fact that God's Word is living and active means that reading God's Word is always meant to be a personal experience. God's Word is not just dead words on a page—it is page after page of living, powerful words—so get ready, because the time you spend studying the Bible in this *Engaging God's Word* course will be life-transforming!

Why Study the Bible?

Some Christians read the Bible because they know they're supposed to. It's a good thing to do, and God expects it. And all that's true! However, there are many additional reasons to study God's Word. Here are just some of them.

We get to know God through His Word. Our God is a relational God who knows us and wants us to know Him. The Scriptures, which He authored, reveal much about Him: how He thinks and feels, what His purposes are, what He thinks about us, how He views the world He made, what He has planned for the future. The Bible shows us God's many attributes—His kindness, goodness, justice, love, faithfulness, mercy, compassion, creativity, redemption, sovereignty, and so on. As we get to know Him through His Word, we come to love and trust Him.

God speaks to us through His Word. One of the primary ways God speaks to us is through His written Word. Don't be surprised if, as you read the Bible, certain parts nearly jump off the page at you, almost as if they'd been written with you in mind. God is the Author of this incredible book, so that's not just possible, it's likely! Whether it is to find comfort, warning, correction, teaching, or guidance, always approach God's Word with your spiritual ears open (Isaiah 55:3) because God, your loving heavenly Father, has things He wants to say to you.

God's Word brings life. Just about everyone wants to learn the secret to "the good life." And the good news is, that secret is found in God's Word. Don't think of the Bible as a bunch of rules. Viewing it with that mindset is a distortion. God gave us His Word because as our Creator and the Creator of the universe, He alone knows how life was meant to work. He knows that love makes us happier than hate, that generosity brings more joy than greed, and that integrity allows us to rest more peacefully at night than deception does. God's ways are not always "easiest" but they are the way to life. As the Psalmist says, *"If Your law had not been my delight, I would have perished in my affliction. I will never forget Your precepts, for by them You have given me life"* (Psalm 119:92-93).

God's Word offers stability in an unstable world. Truth is an ever-changing negotiable for many people in our culture today. But building your life on constantly changing "truth" is like building your house on shifting sand. God's Word, like God Himself, never changes. What He says was true yesterday, is true today, and will still be true a billion years from now. Jesus said, *"Everyone then who hears these words of Mine and does them will be like a wise man who built his house on the rock"* (Matthew 7:24).

God's Word helps us to pray effectively. When we read God's Word and get to know what He is really like, we understand better how to pray. God answers prayers that are according to His will. We discover His will by reading the Bible. First John 5:14-15 tells us that *"this is the confidence that we have toward Him, that if we ask anything according to His will He hears us. And if we know that He hears us in whatever we ask, we know that we have the requests that we have asked of Him."*

How to Get the Most out of *Engaging God's Word*

Each *Engaging God's Word* study contains key elements that have been carefully designed to help you get the most out of your time in God's Word. Slightly modified for your study-at-home success, this approach is very similar to the tried-and-proven Bible study method that Community Bible Study has used with thousands of men, women, and children across the United States and around the world for nearly 40 years. There are some basic things you can expect to find in each course in this series.

❖ Lesson 1 provides an overview of the Bible book (or books) you will study and questions to help you focus, anticipate, and pray about what you will be learning.

❖ Every lesson contains questions to answer on your own, commentary that reviews and clarifies the passage, and three special sections called "Apply what you have learned," "Think about" and "Personalize this lesson."

❖ Some lessons contain memory verse suggestions.

Whether you plan to use *Engaging God's Word* on your own or with a group, here are some suggestions that will help you enjoy and receive the most benefit from your study.

Spread out each lesson over several days. Your *Engaging God's Word* lessons were designed to take a week to complete. Spreading out your study rather than doing it all at once allows time for the things God is teaching you to sink in and for you to practice applying them.

Pray each time you read God's Word. The Bible is a book unlike any other because God Himself inspired it. The same Spirit who inspired the human authors who wrote it will help you to understand and apply it if you ask Him to. So make it a practice to ask Him to make His Word come alive to you every time you read it.

Read the whole passage covered in the lesson. Before plunging into the questions, take time to read the specific chapter or verses that will be covered in that lesson. Doing this will give you important context for the whole lesson. Reading the Bible in context is an important principle in interpreting it accurately.

Begin learning the memory verse. Learning Scripture by heart requires discipline, but the rewards far outweigh the effort. Memorizing a verse allows you to recall it whenever you need it—for personal encouragement and direction, or to share with someone else. Consider writing the verse on a sticky note or index card that you can post where you will see it often or carry with you to review during the day. Reading and re-reading the verse often—out loud when possible—is a simple way to commit it to memory.

Re-read the passage for each section of questions. Each lesson is divided into sections so that you study one small part of Scripture at a time. Before attempting to answer the questions, review the verses that the questions will cover.

Answer the questions without consulting the Commentary or other reference materials. There is great joy in having the Holy Spirit teach you God's Word on your own, without the help of outside resources. Don't cheat yourself of the delight of discovery by reading the Commentary prematurely. Wait until after you've completed the lesson.

Repeat the process for all the question sections.

Prayerfully consider the "Apply what you have learned," marked with the 📌 push pin symbol. The vision of Community Bible Study is not to just gain knowledge about the Bible, but to be transformed by it. For this reason, each set of questions closes with a section that encourages you to apply what you are learning. Usually this section involves action—something for you to do. As you practice these suggestions, your life will change.

Read the Commentary. *Engaging God's Word* commentaries are written by theologians whose goal is to help you understand the context of what you are studying as it relates to the rest of Scripture, God's character, and what the passage means for your life. Of necessity, the commentaries include the author's interpretations. While interesting and helpful, keep in mind that the Commentary is simply one person's understanding of what these passages mean. Other godly men and women have views that are also worth considering.

Pause to contemplate each "Think about" section, marked with the ⬜ notepad symbol. These features, embedded in the Commentary, offer a place to pause and consider some of the principles being brought out by the text. They provide excellent ideas to journal about or to discuss with other believers, especially those doing the study with you.

Jot down insights or prayer points from the "Personalize this lesson" marked with the ☑ check box symbol. While the "Apply what you have learned" section focuses on doing, the "Personalize this lesson" section focuses on becoming. Spiritual transformation is not just about doing right things and refraining from doing wrong things—it is about changing from the inside out. To be transformed means letting God change our hearts so that our attitudes, emotions, desires, reactions, and goals are increasingly like Jesus'. Often this section will discuss something that you cannot do in your own strength—so your response will usually be something to pray about. Remember that becoming more Christ-like is not just a matter of trying harder—it requires God's empowerment.

The Book of Beginnings

God is not in the habit of arguing—He has no need to do so. So when He inspired His servant Moses to write the book of beginnings—this book we call Genesis—He had him write it in a straightforward manner, with no arguments, no attempts to persuade: *"In the beginning, God created the heavens and the earth."* That's just the way it is, period. No human mind could compose a sentence that is at once so simple and so profound. The simple substance of Genesis sets the stage for all that follows throughout the Bible. Profound truths simply stated.

In this introductory book of the Bible we will see the following key events:

- ❖ God creating the heavens, the earth, all plants and creatures, and all that is necessary to sustain life
- ❖ God creating humans (in His image) in a glorious garden
- ❖ God giving humans the choice to obey or disobey Him
- ❖ Humans choosing to disobey and the resultant fall from grace
- ❖ God promising a coming Savior
- ❖ A great flood destroying all but eight humans
- ❖ God choosing to bring His Savior through the lineage of a man named Abraham
- ❖ Abraham's descendants being enslaved in Egypt

We may choose to believe or disbelieve the simple record of these events; God will not argue with us. Jesus chose to believe the Genesis record (Matthew 19:4-5; Mark 1:44; Luke 10:12; and many more).

1. Why do you think many people discount the book of Genesis as a collection of myths?

    _____

    _____

    _____

2. Why do you think Jesus interpreted the Genesis stories as real?

    _____

    _____

    _____

3. What differences could your choice of how to read Genesis make in your life?

    _____

    _____

    _____

If, in the past, you have begun reading the Bible but struggled with skepticism, will you ask God, this time, to reveal to you what He wants you to see and know? If you have never read the Bible, will you ask God to lead you, to help you read this story of beginnings with an open heart and mind? If you are a seasoned and faithful Bible student about to begin anew in studying the book of beginnings, will you ask God to open your spiritual eyes to new vistas of revelation that will magnify your love for and devotion to the Savior revealed in its pages?

The Book of Beginnings

Genesis serves as the grand gateway into God's Word: Creation, rebellion, judgment, and forgiveness are showcased. The book describes the origins of the Hebrew nation, the people through whom God would bring the Messiah, His instrument of salvation.

Think about life's ultimate questions. In an increasingly despairing and rootless society, many feel an urgency to find answers to questions like "Why am I here?" Be prepared to find those answers in this incredible book. Genesis unfolds the remarkable plan of a loving Creator God who designed us with a purpose. It provides a solid basis for hope—in our world's Creator and Redeemer.

Authorship

The Bible claims that Moses, the Hebrew lawgiver and prophet, wrote the book of Genesis (Joshua 8:31; Ezra 7:6; Daniel 9:13). Guided by the Holy Spirit, Moses received much of its content directly from God and added information from documents and oral tradition. As recorded in the New Testament (Matthew 19:7-8; Mark 1:44; John 5:45-46), Jesus plainly states that Moses was the author of the Bible's first five books, called *the Torah*, meaning *the Law*.

Date

Moses was born about 1525 BC and died about 120 years later. The book opens with the creation of the world and ends with Joseph's death in the late 19th-century BC. The exact date of Creation cannot be determined. The 50 chapters of Genesis are highly compressed—especially the first 11, which cover many centuries. The book does not claim to be a history of the world, but focuses on the origins of the Hebrew nation, through which God would bring His Redeemer into the world.

Outline

The first 11 chapters of Genesis are a "primeval history," describing the very beginning of human experience. They focus on matters that touch the human race as a whole and center around four great events: Creation, the Fall, the Great Flood, and the Tower of Babel. The last 39 chapters of Genesis are "patriarchal history" and focus on four central figures: Abraham, Isaac, Jacob, and Joseph (the patriarchs of the Hebrew people). They may be described as a collection of theological biographies.

Jesus Christ in Genesis

The name of Jesus Christ does not appear in the text of Genesis. As the second person of the Trinity, however, He has always existed. The apostle John points out, *"In the beginning was the Word, and the Word was with God, and the Word was God. He was in the beginning with God. All things were made through Him, and without Him was not any thing made that was made"* (1:1-3). The Creator who appears in the opening chapters of Genesis is Jesus Christ Himself, acting in the days before He *"became flesh and dwelt among us"* (John 1:14). Christ also appears as *"the Angel of the LORD"* (Genesis 22:11, 15). God enters His own drama to affirm His love for creatures who have, sadly, declared their independence from Him. In time, He will enter the womb of a Hebrew maiden to become the Redeemer and to offer Himself as a sacrifice for sins. The apostle Paul notes the strong likeness between Adam and Jesus. Jesus came to undo—and much more than undo—the damage done by Adam (Romans 5:9-19).

Crucial Themes in Genesis

People sometimes scoff at the Genesis description as a primitive explanation of the origin of the universe. Yet, as its designer, God speaks His Word into it, and created things spring into being. Genesis explains that the world is filled with troubles because humanity, the pinnacle of creation, rebelled against their Creator. Since the time when humanity first defied Him (Genesis 3), God has been seeking to reclaim His authority in their hearts, which is achieved only when people submit their wills to Him. God woos rather than crushes, urging the rebels home. Sadly, humanity draws no connection between its fallenness and its distress. The Creator permits heartaches and disappointments so we can see our own incompleteness and turn back to the One who gives us life.

Beginning at chapter 12, God takes the initiative and reveals Himself to one man. From that moment, the world begins to move toward a grand climax of redemption. Sacrifice forms another major theme in Genesis. Once humanity rebels and is removed from the Garden of Eden, the Creator shows that the blood of an innocent animal substitute can cover sin's curse. The principle will emerge repeatedly in Genesis and in the rest of Scripture, reaching its height in the Gospels, when Jesus comes personally to serve as God's sacrificial Lamb, the perfect and final sacrifice for sin (Romans 6:23).

Purposes of Genesis

The book gives the historical setting for God's covenant with Israel and describes His character. It separates *Yahweh*, Israel's God, from the strange gods pagans worship. Further, it explains human nature by describing man's original condition, and then relating how he rebelled and continued to do so. Finally, the book shows how God prepares His people for the covenant He later establishes with them (seen in the book of Exodus). In Egypt, however, God allows Israel's condition as a nation of slaves to deteriorate to the point where their need of Him is impossible to ignore.

Genesis and Origins

Broadly speaking, science and Genesis approach the answers to the question of the origins of the universe differently. Many scientists accept the Genesis Creation account, but others believe that the universe originated by chance. Science deals with what may be observed, recorded, measured, weighed, and tested. The Bible insists that the world began by God, who is separate from His creation. This places the matter of origins outside the scope of what is generally considered science. Scientists can yield to personal biases just as readily as non-scientists.

Personalize this lesson.

Genesis is far more than the biblical account of how the world began. It is that, but it also records the first marriage, the first family, the first rebellion against God, and sin's tragic consequences. We will read of the first dysfunctional family—and incidentally, that first family failed in a perfect environment. We'll read about the first murder and the wickedness of a culture trying to function without God's guidelines. Later, we'll see how God chooses a "people of promise." It is almost impossible to imagine a more relevant study. Do you know of a family touched by rebellion, sexual immorality, divorce, drug use? Perhaps it is your own. Genesis will challenge us to respond personally in the world of the 21st century. Consider how you might accept the challenge.

The Creation
Genesis 1:1-2:3

Memorize God's Word: Genesis 1:1.

❖ Genesis 1:1-2—Creation: The Prologue

1. What do these verses tell us about the origin of the universe?

    _____

    _____

    _____

2. According to these verses, who was present at Creation?

    _____

    _____

3. What further details does the Bible give us about Creation in John 1:1-3, 14; Colossians 1:15-17; and Hebrews 1:1-2?

    _____

    _____

    _____

    _____

4. What truth about the Trinity do these passages suggest?

    _____

    _____

    _____

❖ Genesis 1:3-31—Creation: The First Six Days

5. Why do you think the earth is the main focus of the Creation account, since it is so small in size compared with all of creation?

    _____

    _____

6. According to verse 2, what was the condition of the earth?

    _____

    _____

7. What did God create each day?

    _____

    _____

8. How did God initiate and complete each step of creation? (See also Psalm 33:6, 9; Hebrews 11:3.)

    _____

    _____

9. How does the purpose God ascribed to the sun, moon, and stars at Creation contradict popular beliefs concerning astrology and horoscopes?

    _____

    _____

10. a. According to Isaiah 40:26, what response should the heavenly bodies evoke in us?

    _____

    _____

    b. What does Deuteronomy 4:19 and 18:10-13 say about those who misinterpret their purpose and look to these bodies for guidance?

    _____

    _____

11. What unique distinction makes humanity the "crown" of God's creation?

_____

_____

12. What does Psalm 139:13-14 tell us about God's involvement in creating each individual?

_____

_____

_____

13. Because of each human's inherent worth, how should you view yourself and others, including the unborn, the aged, and the impaired?

_____

_____

_____

14. What responsibility does God give humanity concerning the earth?

_____

_____

❖ Genesis 2:1-3—Creation: The Seventh Day

15. Why did God later designate this particular day as *holy* (*set apart*) for His people, Israel? (See Exodus 31:12-17.)

_____

_____

_____

16. How could Isaiah 58:13-14 help us use the Sabbath (whichever day you believe it to be) more effectively?

_____

_____

❖ Genesis 1:1-2:3—Reflections on the God of Creation

17. Re-read Genesis 1:1-2:3. What have you learned about God from these verses?

18. What does the fact that God existed before time and space, and therefore is not bound by either, mean to you?

19. What do you think it means that God created us *"in His own image"*?

20. How should this extraordinary concept affect our daily lives?

Apply what you have learned. How do you think what you have studied so far relates to current scientific information and theories? The "big bang" theory promotes the idea of a sudden, cataclysmic beginning of the universe. This could coincide with the Genesis report of a specific time of beginning. The "intelligent design" theory presupposes a Designer who set the universe in motion with a specific design and plan in mind, which correlates with the Genesis report of God initiating and completing creation. If science and faith don't seem to line up, let's not assume the Bible is mistaken, but rather that science hasn't yet discovered enough to fully corroborate what God's Word says with finality: *"In the beginning, God created the heavens and the earth"* (Genesis 1:1).

The Creation
Genesis 1:1-2:3

The Bible does not argue for God's existence except by pointing to the presence of the universe itself. The Bible often states that the world proclaims the Creator's glory (Psalm 19:1-4; Romans 1:20). Many interpreters understand Genesis 1:1 to be a topic sentence, summarizing the entire Creation account. The rest of chapter 1, according to this view, provides the details of how creation occurred.

Creation Summary

Genesis 1:1 rejects *atheism*, because God is present before the created universe is formed. It denies *pantheism*, since God is separate from His creation. It contradicts *naturalism*, because it asserts that matter is not eternal. In the Bible, the Hebrew verb translated *created—bara*—is used only of divine activity. God does something that He alone can do: He brings into existence a universe that is fully functional, self-sustaining, and filled with testimony about Him. Only God can *bara*—create matter by His spoken word. Popularized in the 1800s, another view of the first two verses is the *Gap Theory*. This view says that the earth was inhabited either by angels (including Satan), or by human beings, or both, in a creation that may have lasted millions of years. However, God found it necessary to punish their rebellion by destroying this creation.

Genesis 1:1-2 and Pagan "Creation Accounts"

Critics like to point out similarities between Genesis 1–2 and other cultures' stories of origins, suggesting that the Genesis author borrowed his material from earlier pagan accounts. Close scrutiny of the pagan accounts of origins reveals strong differences with Genesis. These pagan accounts describe beings that already exist alongside the creator deity. The Bible explains that Moses received truth directly from God: *"With* [Moses] *I speak mouth to mouth, clearly, and not in riddles"* (Numbers 12:8).

The Six Days of Creative Work

Days One, Two, and Three explain that God gives shape to the formlessness. Days Four, Five, and Six relate how He fills the emptiness. Christians have long disagreed on the length of the creative days. The three most-proposed answers are as follows: (1) 24-Hour Day View. The days of Genesis 1 are 24 hours in length, and signs of layering found in the earth's crust are the result of the Flood of Genesis 6–9; (2) Day-Age View—this is a second view, commonly held since the mid-19th-century. This view understands the days of Genesis 1 as epochs of great length, typically millions of years. Advocates of this view point out that the word *yom* can and does sometimes mean a long period of time; (3) Literal Days with Intervening Ages—this third view is a combination of the first two. Here the days of Genesis were 24 hours in length; however, while the creative process took place in these brief spurts, God waited for thousands or millions of years between the days.

Think about the age of the earth. Our increasing knowledge about the solar system challenges our ideas about the age of the universe. Yet the biblical account of Creation is the standard against which everything must be measured. Though theories abound, the Bible does not tell us when the act of Creation took place, nor does it give an indisputable statement about how long it took. We can easily get so caught up in the details that we miss the majesty, the wonder of it all. God took a great formless void—a vast emptiness—and created this incredibly complex world in which we live. And He did it all with the power of His Word. He simply spoke the world into existence.

God began by bringing into existence light, which is an expression of His own character (1 John 1:5). The second day saw the separation of the skies from the waters. The third day brought the boundaries of earthly seas from dry land. On the fourth day, God placed the sun, moon, and stars into the sky. On the fifth day, the water was filled with vast varieties of sea creatures and the sky with every kind of bird. On the sixth day, God created the animals and—the crown of His creative work—humanity.

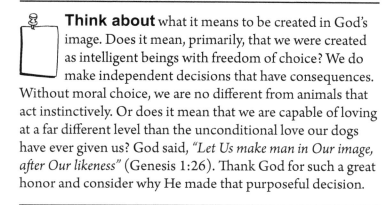

Think about what it means to be created in God's image. Does it mean, primarily, that we were created as intelligent beings with freedom of choice? We do make independent decisions that have consequences. Without moral choice, we are no different from animals that act instinctively. Or does it mean that we are capable of loving at a far different level than the unconditional love our dogs have ever given us? God said, *"Let Us make man in Our image, after Our likeness"* (Genesis 1:26). Thank God for such a great honor and consider why He made that purposeful decision.

Man is created as a combination of body and spirit; he is by nature a dependent being, unlike God, who is self-sustaining. Apart from God supplying his daily needs, mankind cannot continue.

Genesis 1 identifies the Creator as *Elohim* (God), a plural noun with a singular verb called *a plural of majesty*, suggesting God's complex makeup. The proposal to create man (verse 26) also uses two plural forms: *"Let Us make man in Our image."* All three persons of the triune Godhead are involved in Creation. God creates; the Holy Spirit hovers; and Jesus Christ plays a major role. Colossians 1:16 declares, *"By Him all things were created."* The Trinity's involvement cannot be disputed, nor will it be fully understood this side of heaven.

The Seventh Day of Joy and Reflection

On the day after creating man, God rested and did no work, as an example for His covenant people. God placed a special blessing on the seventh day and set it apart—*"made it holy"* (2:3). The seventh day would become known as the *Sabbath*, from the Hebrew word meaning *to cease.* By connecting the Sabbath day with God's creative work, Moses taught the Israelites that the days of work followed by a day of rest and refreshment was God's gracious gift.

Personalize this lesson.

✓ Genesis tells its readers that God created the heavens, the earth, and all living things. It provides a few, but not many, details about how He created. Ever since, people have had differing views about how to fill in the blanks of those specifics—and even how to interpret the words that are there. But, rather than arguing over the specifics of the macro-creation, why not focus on the application of the micro-creation—on your own individual life, among the billions of earth's inhabitants. Jesus once counseled His listeners, *"How can you say to your brother, 'Let me take the speck out of your eye,' when there is the log in your own eye? You hypocrite, first take the log out of your own eye, and then you will see clearly to take the speck out of your brother's eye"* (Matthew 7:4-5). In other words, I need to evaluate and correct my own beliefs and behaviors before I judge the beliefs and behaviors of others. Will you ask God to use this Genesis study to help you evaluate your own life and to increasingly conform it to His wishes?

The Fellowship and Fall of Man
Genesis 2:4-3:24

Memorize God's Word: Genesis 3:15.

❖ Genesis 2:4-25—Life Before the Fall

1. What kind of home did the Lord provide for the first man?

   _____

   _____

   _____

2. What assignment did God give the man at this time?

   _____

   _____

   _____

3. What does this tell you about our need for purpose and meaningful activity?

   _____

   _____

4. In the midst of such abundance, what one thing in the garden did God say was "off limits"? Why do you think God gave man this restriction?

   _____

   _____

   _____

5. Even though Adam lived in a perfect environment, what did
    God say was missing in his life?

    _____

    _____

6. The Hebrew word translated *helper* in Genesis 2:18 occurs 21
    times in the Old Testament. Look for this word, translated *help*
    in the ESV, in Psalm 33:20 and 70:5. To whom does this word
    refer in these verses?

    _____

    _____

❖ Genesis 3:1-7—The Fall of Mankind

7. Who spoke through the serpent in this passage? (See
    Revelation 12:9.)

    _____

    _____

8. What does the Bible tell us about this being? (See John 8:44;
    1 Peter 5:8.)

    _____

    _____

    _____

9. What tactics does the tempter use to make the forbidden fruit
    seem so desirable?

    _____

    _____

10. What should the woman have done when the serpent began to
    challenge God's words and motives? (See James 4:7.) What did
    she do instead?

    _____

    _____

11. What desires did the forbidden fruit stir up in the woman? (See 1 John 2:15-17.)

_____

_____

12. How can we guard against these same things controlling us? (See Romans 6:11-14.)

_____

_____

13. What additional defenses has God given us in our fight against temptation? (See Romans 8:8-9; 1 Corinthians 10:13; Hebrews 2:18.)

_____

_____

❖ Genesis 3:8-24—Life After the Fall

14. What were the first results of sin for Adam and Eve? What did they do about it? (See also Genesis 3:7.)

_____

_____

15. What is the significance of God seeking them?

_____

_____

16. Who does Adam blame for his sin? Who does Eve blame? Who does God blame? (See Romans 5:12-14.)

_____

_____

17. What should we all do as quickly as possible when we know that we've sinned? (See 1 John 1:8-9.)

_____

_____

18. What does the curse God pronounced against the serpent in Genesis 3:15 refer to? (See Hebrews 2:14-15.)

_____

_____

19. What did Adam and Eve's sin destroy? What did it introduce into the world?

_____

_____

20. What is the significance of God's action in Genesis 3:21? What does this foreshadow? (See John 1:29; Hebrews 9:22.)

_____

_____

Apply what you have learned. The consequences of Adam and Eve's sin are overwhelming. Their spiritual death brought separation from intimate fellowship with God and banishment from the Garden of Eden. These consequences far outweighed any momentary pleasure Adam and Eve might have felt in biting into that tempting fruit. Satan's temptations are clever; he is a master at hooking us with his inviting deception. Pray daily that the Lord will open your spiritual eyes to recognize how sin always divides and separates. Most especially it banishes us from the Eden of fellowship with the Savior. Nothing is worth that! When temptation comes, join the Psalmist in his prayer: "*A day in Your courts is better than a thousand elsewhere. I would rather be a doorkeeper in the house of my God than dwell in the tents of wickedness*" (Psalm 84:10).

The Fellowship and Fall of Man
Genesis 2:4-3:24

Chapters 2 and 3 focus in particular on mankind's moral responsibilities as well as the biblical explanation of how sin spoiled the first people's ideal life. When God comes gently seeking His wayward creatures, His rebuke is kind, but direct. Along with His declarations concerning the penalties for sin, He also speaks of a day when another Human will enter the world and defeat the tempter.

The Setting of Humanity's Probation

In chapter 2, we see God forming man from dust and breathing life into him. To provide a place for Adam and Eve, God *"planted a garden in Eden, in the east"* (2:8)—the setting for mankind's moral test.

The name Eden was given to the garden's region that lay at the headwaters of four rivers. On modern maps, the names of two of these rivers, the Tigris and the Euphrates, appear in the Mesopotamian Valley (modern Iraq). It is likely that the Flood altered earth's topography; attempts to locate the original Garden of Eden have proven fruitless.

The Fellowship of Humanity's Probation

Adam communed with God, but his moral condition had not been tested. That test emerges here in the form of a tree, *"the tree of the knowledge of good and evil"* (2:17). It alone is off-limits for mankind. The results of violating that restriction are grave: Death would result.

God recognized man's one great lack in Eden and saw that it was *"not good that the man should be alone"* (2:18). Spouses would fulfill the need for companionship and encouragement. God then fashions a woman to serve as Adam's mate, to be cherished and treasured as a partner.

The Fall of Humanity

Misery and destruction now enter human experience through a serpent, Satan—the real villain. Satan presents his temptation to Eve as an advantage. He questions God's goodness: *"Did God actually say, 'You shall not eat of any tree in the garden'?"* (Genesis 3:1). According to Satan, if God really cared about Adam and Eve, He would want them to share in the bounty of all His trees. Eve expands God's single command and adds words that God never spoke: *"Neither shall you touch it"* (Genesis 3:3). Scripture declares the danger of adding to and subtracting from God's commandments (Deuteronomy 4:2; Revelation 22:18-19). Satan then challenges God's righteousness, *"You will not surely die"* (Genesis 3:4). The devil still uses this line of reasoning today. Adam and Eve simply want more than they have, and they especially want to be like God. Since that time, humanity has been repeating this pattern of being independent from God, but God can give His creatures nothing better than Himself. Instead of becoming wise, they bring disaster, sin, and misery into the world.

Think about the human need for companionship. Even though Adam lived in a beautiful paradise and enjoyed daily conversations with God, something was missing. God created Eve so that she and Adam could experience intimate relationship and share in each other's lives. From the very beginning, God desired His people to live in community and value relationships. With His gift of Eve to Adam, He not only provided the world's first model of marriage, but populated the earth with people as well. If you are married, how might these verses inspire you to appreciate your spouse? Whether you are married or not, are you encouraged knowing that God doesn't expect you to "go it alone"? How can God's intention for relationships motivate you as you invest in the family and friends He has given you to share your life with?

The Decree Against Mankind

With grace, God woos Adam and Eve back to Himself in their godly sorrow and repentance. First, He reminds them about the penalties for their sin. Adam lays the blame for his sin on Eve and, indirectly, on God

Himself. God also confronts her to establish her part in the event. Eve passes the responsibility on to the serpent (Genesis 3:13). While she ate the forbidden fruit first, God holds Adam accountable for transgression, because he knew what he was doing.

God now pronounces judgment on these three creatures. The lowest physical posture—crawling—reflects the serpent's part in bringing sin into the world. However, God will one day bring a Human Being into the world who will deal with Satan. The tempter will strike Him a dangerous, but temporary blow to the heel. The Redeemer, on the other hand, will crush Satan's head and finally defeat him. Eve can expect a life that includes pain, especially in childbearing. Another part of the penalty is found in the words, *"Your desire shall be for your husband."* Not just sexual, this is a desire to dominate, as its use in Genesis 4:7 makes clear. Before she fell, Eve was content in her marriage. Now, although she may want to dominate her mate, he will often exercise his will over her, and not always in a way that benefits her.

God's pronouncement against Adam involves not only the man, but also the very ground itself. Note that work forms no part of the divine curse. God told Adam to cultivate and tend the garden before the Fall. Work is part of God's blessing, but after Adam and Eve's rebellion, labor becomes inefficient. Thorns, thistles, and sweat become part of human experience. Above all looms the shadow of death. Because of the Fall, mankind will suffer the penalty God has foretold.

Salvation Beyond the Fall

In place of the fig-leaf garments they had devised, God gives Adam and Eve garments of skin. This new clothing requires the sacrificial death of an animal. While He was completing such an action, the Lord likely explained that atonement requires a substitutionary death—a principle that carries through the entire Bible. The more pressing issue at the moment is the necessity of excluding Adam and Eve from the garden. They still have access to the Tree of Life if they stay in Eden, which would give them the ability to live forever in their fallen condition (3:22), effectively destroying any hope of redemption. To make doubly sure that the couple cannot re-enter the garden, God places special angels and a flaming sword to block the entrance to mankind's original home. God displays His grace by not allowing their fallen condition to become permanent.

Personalize this lesson.

☑ What is your relationship with God? Are you hiding from Him because you have sinned? Clearly, you are not the first person to disobey God's Word. Adam and Eve did it way back in the beginning, and in all human history only one Man ever went through an entire lifetime free of sin. Paul wrote, *"All have sinned and fall short of the glory of God."* Likewise, all have had a natural tendency to try to hide their sins from the all-seeing God. Why attempt the impossible tasks of trying either to live a sinless life or to hide your sins from God? Why not quickly answer Him when He calls out, asking where you've gone? Why not accept the covering He has provided for the shame of your sin? (See Philippians 3:9.) If you have hidden your shame from God, will you come out of hiding and accept His covering, and let Him change you rather than futilely trying to become clean enough to present yourself to Him?

Lesson 4

Where Rebellion Leads, Part 1
Genesis 4:1-6:4

Memorize God's Word: Genesis 5:1b.

❖ Genesis 4:1-16—Rebellion Leads to Murder and Sorrow

1. What do verses 1-5 tell us about Cain and Abel?

   _____

   _____

2. Why did they bring offerings to the Lord?

   _____

   _____

3. According to Hebrews 11:4, 6, why did God accept Abel's offering, but not Cain's?

   _____

   _____

4. Why did Cain kill his brother?

   _____

   _____

5. Trace the downward steps Scripture refers to as *"the way of Cain"* (Jude 11).

   a. Genesis 4:5_____

   _____

  b. Genesis 4:8 _____

   _____

  c. Genesis 4:9 _____

   _____

  d. Genesis 4:16 _____

   _____

 6. What warning for yourself do you see in this passage?

  _____

  _____

 7. What evidence of God's grace do you see in His dealings with Cain?

  _____

  _____

❖ Genesis 4:17-5:5—Rebellion Leads to Hostility

 8. What effects of sin's entrance into the world do you see in this passage?

  _____

  _____

 9. What cultural developments took place during this period?

  _____

  _____

 10. How did Eve experience God's comfort after Abel's death?

  _____

  _____

 11. How has God comforted you in difficult times?

  _____

  _____

12. What positive report on mankind does this passage record?

_____

_____

❖ Genesis 5—Rebellion Leads to Death

13. According to Genesis 5:1-4, how were men and women born after the Fall (Genesis 3) different from God's original creation?

_____

_____

_____

14. What is the significance of this difference? (See Galatians 5:17.)

_____

_____

15. What repetitive phrase does the writer use in chapter 5 to emphasize the ultimate, unavoidable consequence of sin? How many times do you find this phrase in this chapter?

_____

_____

16. What commentary does Paul make on this consequence in Romans 5:12 and 6:23?

_____

_____

17. One man escaped this consequence of sin. Who is he, and what does this passage tell us about him?

_____

_____

18. What else do Hebrews 11:5 and Jude 14-15 tell us about this man?

_____

_____

❖ Genesis 6:1-4—Rebellion Leads to Corruption

19. What was God's response to man's sin and rebellion culminating in the intermarriage of the *"sons of God"* and the *"daughters of man"*? How many *"years of grace"* did He allow until the Flood?

_____

_____

20. In Hebrew, the word Nephilim (Genesis 6:4) means *fallen ones,* which is evidently how God viewed them. How did other people view unusual race? (See also Numbers 13:31-33.)

_____

_____

21. How does our culture reflect the same kinds of corruption and rebellion against God described in the passage we studied this week?

_____

_____

Apply what you have learned. The vast difference between how God created humanity: *"in the likeness of God"* (Genesis 5:1) and how Adam's descendants were born *"in his own likeness, after his image"* (5:3) is a sad commentary on the faulty spiritual DNA handed down through the generations. Sin has flawed us. But wait—there's good news! Christ paid the penalty for our sin. We must ask God in order to receive the forgiveness made available to all by the substitutionary death of Christ. Have you taken advantage of God's solution to the problem created by our very first parents? Why not surrender your will to the Lord right now and receive Christ into your life? If you already have trusted Christ as your Savior, why not surrender your will to the Lord daily to experience the inner peace that comes with loving obedience?

Where Rebellion Leads, Part 1
Genesis 4:1-6:4

Expelled from the Garden of Eden, man soon discovers his terrible blunder. Murder, sorrow, hostility, and death plague Adam and his descendants. Exceptions occur, and the faithfulness of Abel, Enoch, and Noah will set them apart from the rest of humanity.

Murder and Sorrow

Eve names her first child Cain. She bears other children, but only Abel is mentioned here by name.

God makes coverings from animal skins to provide their clothing. We can assume that when God killed these animals, He instructed Adam and Eve on the need for blood sacrifice for redemption. Cain and Abel understood sacrifice to be an essential part of worship. Abel's offering includes portions from a firstborn animal of his flock. Cain brings an offering of vegetables or grain.

God finds pleasure in Abel's offering, but not in Cain's. It appears that the problem with Cain's offering is his attitude. Cain may have made his offering grudgingly, resenting God's claims on his possessions.

Cain then becomes angry and depressed. Being angry or rebellious with God places us in a position of hopelessness and depression. God wants to prevent the negative effects of Cain's anger, knowing it will bring destruction if left unchecked. He confronts Cain to help him face his condition. If Cain should choose to *"do well"* (4:7), his gifts will be acceptable. Instead, Cain murders his brother. God casts him out of his family's home and land and decrees that his future attempts at farming will be futile, making him *"a wanderer on the earth"* (4:12).

Think about accepting the consequences of our choices. Cain said to the Lord, *"My punishment is greater than I can bear"* (4:13). Cain ruined his life because he let his emotions control him. Yet God is merciful to Cain, even in his sin. If we make a wrong choice, are we doomed to be *"wanderer[s]"*? No. We can turn to God, and He will give us strength to endure the problem we have created. He will even forgive us for our sin and cleanse us from all unrighteousness (1 John 1:9). However, the consequences usually remain.

Cain finds God's penalties *"greater than [he can] bear"* (4:13). His primary fear is of punishment by the community. His response to God indicates that he has other siblings or relatives, and that they would avenge Abel. Punishment or justice at the time was the responsibility of the nearest male relative, who measured it out according to the crime. To prevent him from being killed, God *"put a mark on Cain"* (4:15) to warn others away. This may have been a physical mark of some kind, or some token of God's reassurance that Cain would survive.

Hostility

Banished, Cain goes *"away from the presence of the Lord"* (4:16) and chooses to live in the land of Nod (means *wandering* or *homelessness*). Cain defies God's curse to be a *"wanderer"* (4:12) and builds a city. The mention of Cain's wife raises a question about her origin. The most likely answer is that she is a sister or a niece. (At this time, family lines were not polluted. God did not declare incest to be sin until the Mosaic Law.) Cain's family expands after he begins building his city, Enoch, named after his son. Considerable culture develops there. Lamech, the father of Enoch's entrepreneurs, explains to his wives how he carried out justice. He killed a man for wounding him, but the wounds he inflicted were more severe than those he received, violating the principle of divine justice (Exodus 21:23-25).

Death

The ancestral line in Genesis 5 records a series of unusual life spans. In the pre-Flood era, people routinely lived for 700 years and more. One notable exception in the pre-Flood era is Enoch (not the Enoch mentioned above), in Seth's line, who *"walked with God"* (5:24). Enoch does not undergo death and is taken directly to heaven: *"he was not, for God took him"* (5:24).

Corruption

The prelude to the Flood contains a remarkable set of events. The *"sons of God"* noted the beauty of the *"daughters of man"* (6:1) and took them as wives. The identity of the sons of God is not clear. Students of Genesis generally favor one of two interpretations. The first identifies the sons of God as Seth's line of descent. These men are called *"sons of God"* because of their godliness and spirituality. The *"daughters of man"* are the female descendants of the ungodly line of Cain and lack the spiritual qualities of the men who marry them. Displeased with these mixed marriages and the decline of man, God shortens life spans and, ultimately, brings the judgment of the Flood.

The second interpretation of Genesis 6:1 identifies the *"sons of God"* as fallen angels who have left their heavenly home, lived on the earth, and married human wives. Neither interpretation clearly explains the mysterious *Nephilim* (*fallen ones*), who seem somehow to be around both before and after the Flood (Genesis 6:4), even though Genesis is quite specific about only Noah and his immediate family surviving the Flood. Some commentators describe these mighty men as the offspring of those unholy unions. Why they were not all wiped out in the Flood is unclear. Others suggest that Nephilim describes a people who *fall on* or *overpower* others, picturing the degraded society before the Flood. After the Flood, Nephilim are mentioned in Numbers 13:31-33, where the fearful spies sent into Canaan use the word in a generic sense, describing the people in Canaan as mighty giants (*"stronger than we are ... of great height"*).

Personalize this lesson.

This section of Genesis illustrates how the Fall profoundly changed the way humanity lived. Death is now a certainty, and modern men and women do their best to ignore it and prolong life. A second change is the beginning of a cultured civilization, led by Cain's descendants, who were alienated from God. Cain's people were devoted to the things of this world rather than to God. People who live for this world work harder to fill their empty existence and to silence the fear of death. God's solution to fear of death and living in a fallen civilization is redemption. Jesus Christ has come to redeem us from sin and death. That victory includes release from fear's bondage. He calls on us as redeemed people to redeem the culture in which we live.

Lesson 5

Where Rebellion Leads, Part 2
Genesis 6:5-9:29

Memorize God's Word: Genesis 9:13.

❖ Genesis 6:5-22—The Causes of the Flood

1. What does this passage tell us about the condition of mankind at the time of the Flood?

   _____

   _____

2. What do you learn about God from these verses?

   _____

   _____

   _____

3. How do we know that man's depravity didn't take God by surprise or cause Him to change His plans? (See 1 Samuel 15:29 and Isaiah 46:10.)

   _____

   _____

   _____

4. Why did God spare Noah and his family? (See also Hebrews 11:6-7.)

   _____

   _____

5. What challenges do you think Noah may have faced in building the ark?

    _____

    _____

6. What were the *"events as yet unseen"* spoken of in Hebrews 11:7? (See also Genesis 2:5-6.)

    _____

    _____

7. According to 2 Peter 2:5, what else was Noah doing while he built the ark?

    _____

    _____

8. When have you faced challenges in your efforts to obey God?

    _____

    _____

    _____

❖ Genesis 7:1–8:19—Description of the Flood

9. What does God tell Noah to do when the ark is completed?

    _____

    _____

    _____

10. How is Noah able to accomplish such a monumental task?

    _____

    _____

11. How could this encourage you when God asks you to do something that seems impossible?

    _____

    _____

12. What details does this passage give us about the Flood and its consequences?

_____

_____

13. Do you think the Flood was global? Why or why not?

_____

_____

14. How does Noah determine that the Flood is over?

_____

_____

15. What are God's instructions to Noah after the flood waters dry up?

_____

_____

❖ Genesis 8:20–9:29—The Aftermath of the Flood

16. What is the first thing Noah does after he and his family leave the ark?

_____

_____

17. What does this tell you about Noah?

_____

_____

18. What does Genesis 8:21 reveal about humanity?

_____

_____

19. Describe the covenant that God makes with Noah after the Flood. What does God say will be the sign of this covenant?

_____

_____

20. Has God kept His covenant? Why is this meaningful to you?

_____

_____

21. How does the relationship between people and animals change at this time? (Compare with Genesis 1:28-30.)

_____

_____

22. What restriction does God place on man's new dietary practices? Why? (See also Leviticus 17:11.)

_____

_____

23. How do God's instructions to Noah in Genesis 9:5-6 demonstrate the high value He places on human life?

_____

_____

Apply what you have learned. This lesson shows us how greatly God values human life. Are we, today, insensitive to culturally acceptable violence that damages and devalues people? God treasures the unborn, the old and sick, and even human lives that are harmed or destroyed by scientific experimentation. Many of our culture's ungodly standards go unchallenged by believers. What must our response be? First, we should examine the most unbiased information we can find. Next, measure our culture's answers against the standard of God's answers in His Word. Then stand up for the truth.

Where Rebellion Leads, Part 2
Genesis 6:5-9:29

God determines that He must judge the worldwide rebellion and then repopulate the earth through the offspring of faithful Noah. Noah obeys God's instructions to build a vessel that will house his family and representative pairs of earth's animals. Following the Flood, God blesses Noah's family and tells them to repopulate the earth.

The Flood's Causes

Mankind is steadily decaying. Moses cites man's excessive wickedness and God's knowledge of man's inner makeup. God *"regretted that He had made man on the earth, and it grieved Him to His heart"* (6:6). God resolves to destroy human beings and most of the animal creation. The notable exception is Noah, a man who finds favor with God because of his personal godliness. Noah's perfection lay not in sinlessness, but in his faith (Hebrews 11:7). *"Noah walked with God."* Therefore, God orders Noah to prepare for the coming judgment by building an ark. Only Noah, his family, and a large number of animals would be aboard this vessel.

Think about obedience. When God told Noah to build an ark because a great flood was coming to punish the world's population for their wickedness, Noah obediently began building it according to God's specifications, even though he had never seen rain. Apparently he talked as he worked because we are told he was a preacher of righteousness (2 Peter 2:5). No one heeded his warnings or acknowledged their need for salvation from the judgment to come. Was Noah discouraged? Perhaps, but he is listed in Hebrews 11 as a hero of the faith.

Several things point to the Genesis Flood being of global proportion, not a regional catastrophe: (1) *"All people"* (6:13) were to be destroyed; (2) the waters would rise higher than the mountains; (3) the Flood lasted for over a year (compare 7:6 and 8:13); (4) an ark was required to preserve life, which would have been unnecessary for a local flood; (5) the New Testament affirms that the Genesis Flood was global (2 Peter 3:3-7); (6) the size of the ark makes possible an animal population large enough to repopulate the earth after the destruction.

The Flood's Catastrophe

The enormous ark requires a great deal of time and effort to construct. Eventually, God commands Noah to *"go into the ark"* (Genesis 7:1). The Hebrew text suggests that the translation ought to read, *"Come into the ark."* God is not a detached observer; He would endure the experience along with Noah and his family.

Think about God being with us in our testing. Far from being indifferent, God has promised He will never leave us or forsake us—a promise made in the Old Testament (Deuteronomy 31:6) and repeated in the New Testament (Hebrews 13:5). With Him beside you, you can handle what you thought you couldn't handle and be victorious at the end. He may not change the situation, but He will change you.

Noah takes matched pairs of animals into the ark. Once aboard, *"the LORD shut him in"* (7:16). The flood waters begin to collect. Genesis 7:11 indicates that probably most of the waters came from underground reservoirs—*"all the fountains of the great deep"*—breaking up. Nonstop rain for 40 days added to the supply, but the underground water sources may have continued flooding for as long as 150 days—nearly four months after the rains stopped. Eventually, *"all flesh"* (7:21) perishes.

The Flood continues for five months before the waters begin to recede. The ark touches dry land seven months after the rain first began to fall. For two-and-a-half additional months, the ark rests near the mountaintops while the waters continue to fall. Noah determines the proper time for leaving the ark by sending out birds. On its third try the dove does not return. *"So*

Noah knew that the waters had subsided from the earth" (8:11). Noah and his family are on the ark for about one year. At that point, God directs Noah, his family, and the animals, to *"Go out from the ark"* (8:15-19).

The Flood's Consequences

Noah then builds an altar and sacrifices clean animals on it as thanksgiving. But God now also permits human beings to kill animals for food. To display respect for life, the blood must be drained from any meat that is to be eaten. If a human being takes the life of another human, the guilty person must pay with his or her own life. From God's point of view, human blood must be shed because the life of the murder *victim* is too precious to go unpaid. God seals the Noahic covenant (9:8-17) with the sign of the rainbow (Hebrew, *bow*). What men use for killing, God displays in the heavens as a symbol of peace. God's statement that *"never again will there be a flood to destroy the earth"* points to the flood being worldwide.

The Flood's Survivors

The repopulation of the globe comes entirely from Noah's three sons. Shem would become the father of the Shemitic (or Semitic) peoples, including the Jews; Ham, the father of peoples that include the Egyptians, the Babylonians, and the Canaanites. The descendants of Japheth would spread into central Asia and Europe.

Noah gets drunk and lies uncovered inside his tent. The Bible says, *"Ham, the father of Canaan, saw the nakedness of his father and told his two brothers outside"* (9:22), suggesting that Ham makes his father's shame a conversational topic with his brothers. Shem and Japheth respectfully cover Noah. The seriousness of Ham's actions merits a curse from his father. Noah's curse is specifically against Canaan and his branch of the family, not Ham. The curse is against wickedness and is important to Israelite history because God is revealing the seeds of sin, which brought His command for Israel to destroy Canaan's wicked descendants when Israel entered the Promised Land. Noah's respectful sons, Shem and Japheth, will be blessed. From Shem will come Abraham, the children of Israel and, ultimately, the Messiah. The Japhethites, who will later fill the area north of the Mediterranean, will expand greatly and benefit from Shem's spiritual heritage.

Personalize this lesson.

As the society of Noah's era deteriorated, God finally said, "Enough is enough," and He judged: *"My Spirit shall not abide in man forever"* (Genesis 6:3). How different is that from today? Wickedness is rampant; people *"call evil good and good evil"* (Isaiah 5:20). You may not be able to change the entire corrupt world, but you can be a witness of God to those around you. In recounting the wicked days of Noah, Peter wrote, *"In your hearts honor Christ the Lord as holy, always being prepared to make a defense to anyone who asks you for a reason for the hope that is in you; yet do it with gentleness and respect, having a good conscience, so that, when you are slandered, those who revile your good behavior in Christ may be put to shame"* (1 Peter 3:15-16). What steps can you take to *"honor Christ the Lord as holy"* and to always be *"prepared to make a defense to anyone who asks you for a reason for the hope that is in you"*?

A Lesson Not Learned
Genesis 10–11

❖ Genesis 10—The Spread of the Nations

1. List some of the descendants of each of Noah's sons.

    a. Shem: _____

    _____

    _____

    b. Ham: _____

    _____

    _____

    c. Japheth: _____

    _____

    _____

2. Why has God given us the list of the descendants of Noah's sons?

    _____

    _____

3. According to Noah's prophecy in Genesis 9:24-27, which son's family line will dominate the others?

    _____

4. What will be the relationship between the clans of Shem and Japheth?

    _____

5. What relationship will Shem have with Canaan (Ham's son)?

    _____

6. Read Acts 17:24-28 and refer to Lesson 5. How do we know that the development of these family lines (nations), as well as their time and place in history, isn't accidental?

    _____

    _____

7. Knowing the ultimate purpose for these nations and their boundaries (Acts 17:27), how does this understanding relate to the time and place in which you live?

    _____

    _____

❖ Genesis 11:1-9—The Confusion of Language

8. a. What do the people of Shinar decide to do?

        _____

        _____

    b. Why? _____

        _____

9. How does their determination conflict with God's specific instructions to Noah and his descendants? (See Genesis 9:1, 7.)

    _____

    _____

10. What do their motives and their deliberate disregard of God's command reveal about these people?

    _____

    _____

11. a. How does God respond to their plan? _____

        _____

b. What is the result?_____

_____

12. What evidence of defiance toward God's will do you see in our world today?

_____

_____

❖ Genesis 11:10-32—The Preparation of the Chosen Nation

13. To which family line does the writer of Genesis shift his focus in these verses?

_____

_____

14. What does the inclusion of all the names and details in chapters 10 and 11 tell you about God?

_____

_____

_____

15. According to Acts 7:2-4, where was Abram (later called Abraham) living when he first heard God's call?

_____

16. What does Joshua 24:2 tell us about his family's religious practices at that time?

_____

_____

17. Who accompanied Abram when they first set out to answer God's call? What was their destination?

_____

_____

_____

18. They interrupted their journey and settled in Haran. What do you think prompted Abram to resume his journey and obey God's call? (See Acts 7:4.)

_____

_____

19. What do we know about Abram when he first answered God's call? (See also Hebrews 11:6, 8.)

_____

_____

20. How do you think you would respond if God led you in a definite direction without telling you where it would end? What kind of faith would that require?

_____

_____

Apply what you have learned. Terah was dead long before he died. Spiritually dead, that is. Joshua 24:2 makes clear that he *"served other gods."* Abram had heard God's call to go to the land of God's promise and moved himself and his family out of Ur and in the right direction (Acts 7:2-3). However, under his father Terah's leadership, they went as far as Haran and stopped (Genesis 11:31). The Bible is silent about why they stopped. Certainly Terah slowed down his son, who did not take one step farther on his God-appointed journey until after his father's death (Acts 7:4). Jesus calls us to *"Follow Me"* (Matthew 4:19). Are you stuck in Haran, in any sense? Will you ask God to help you get loose from Haran and resume following Him?

A Lesson Not Learned
Genesis 10–11

Though the Flood's waters have barely receded, people soon show how determined they are to violate God's order to disperse and fill the earth. The post-Flood generation settles on the Mesopotamian plain and begins to build a huge city where they expect their collective actions to exempt them from future disasters. God soon puts an end to their plans by confusing their language. (Note: Chapter 11 precedes chapter 10 chronologically and explains how the situation outlined in chapter 10 arose.) Man's prideful attempt fails; the nations scatter and repopulate the globe. Additionally, the line of people through whom God will bring the Redeemer begins to emerge in Shem's offspring.

The Spread of the Nations

Genesis 10 is often called the "Table of Nations." The chapter emphasizes the common family of humanity from Adam through Noah and his sons and explains God's determination to bless the world through the Hebrew line. The Bible does not recognize the concept of distinct "races," yet Genesis 10 does recognize the differences among Noah's descendants.

Think about scattering and gathering. God scattered the people by confusing their language. Making it virtually impossible for them to communicate, He effectively broke their rebellion against Him. God desires harmony among His people, but He took drastic action to break unity that was being used to dishonor Him and thwart His purpose. In Galatians 3:28, Paul explained God's plan to gather all nations back together again in Christ: *"There is neither Jew nor Greek, there is neither* *slave nor free, there is no male and female, for you are all one in Christ Jesus."* He took dramatic action to restore unity that would be used to honor Him and His Son. He commissioned His church to bring people together.

Chapter 10 gives the names of the offspring of Shem, Ham, and Japheth. Ham's most famous grandchild is named Nimrod, who is called *"a mighty hunter before the LORD."* Nimrod's name means *we shall rebel*. Nimrod founds cities that, in time, become large population centers. In this region, cities band together to form the first great powers built upon plunder and cruelty: the Babylonian and Assyrian Empires.

For the purposes of Genesis, Ham's most important son is Canaan. Cursed in connection with his father's disrespect of Noah, Canaan becomes the father of the people who inhabit the Promised Land when Israel comes out of Egypt. By the time of the Exodus, Canaan's children are notoriously immoral, practicing child sacrifice and ritual prostitution. Moses opens his discussion of the Shemites by noting that Shem is the father of Eber. Eber is the ancestor of Abraham and is most noted for his connection with the term *Hebrew*, meaning *descendant of Eber*.

The Confusion of Languages

Chronologically, Genesis 11:1-9 belongs before chapter 10. Originally, *"the whole earth had one language and the same words."* The population probably settled close to where the ark came to rest, southeast of the Black Sea. Earth's population spreads and moves into the Tigris Valley, a region known as Shinar. They resist God's command to disperse and fill the earth, choosing instead to congregate in a huge city. God knows that if they remain together, their arrogance will be limitless.

Think about making plans that omit God. The population of Shinar chose not to fulfill His purpose for their lives, but they clung to their desire to feel spiritual and reach heaven. Their pride in their efforts and accomplishments was undoubtedly what offended God. They ignored His plan in favor of their own—just as many do today. Spiritual longing is inherent in humanity, but intellectual pride, lifestyle choices, or spiritual deception prevents many of us from seeking or serving God. The New Age movement is really not new at all. God judged it in the land of Shinar long, long ago. The narrow road that leads to life (Matthew 7:14) is not through "self-fulfillment," but through humbly submitting to God's glorious plan for us.

God knows that one expression of rebellion will lead to another: *"Nothing that they propose to do will now be impossible for them"* (11:6). God intervenes with a simple solution. He confuses the language of Shinar's inhabitants and makes communication impossible. The people will be forced to do what they should have done from the beginning. God scatters them over the globe and halts their building of the city, which becomes known as *Babel*. The Hebrew word appears 238 times in the Old Testament and is translated *Babylon* 236 of those times. Only in Genesis 10:10 and 11:9 is the word translated Babel. The word is related to the Hebrew term meaning *to confuse*. The city and its related projects align themselves with the serpent's purpose to confuse and deceive humanity by glorifying man and defying God. Eventually, history will draw to a close with Babylon destroyed (Revelation 18) and the tempter cast into the lake of burning sulfur (Revelation 20:19).

The Preparation of the Chosen Nation

While men challenge divine authority and show themselves worthy of judgment, God moves ahead with His own plans. Abraham, who, beginning in chapter 12 will become the central figure in Genesis, will be God's channel of blessing. His origins are traced through 10 generations from Shem, who began a family two years after the Flood, through Peleg, to Abram. The final stage of preparing the chosen line comes in the family of Terah, who has three sons: Abram, Nahor, and Haran.

This family's original home is *"Ur of the Chaldeans."* The location is uncertain, but the biblical language suggests a location in the northern end of the Mesopotamian valley, because there is no trace of the Chaldeans living in the southern plain for a thousand years after Abraham comes on the scene. God first speaks to Abram while he lives in Ur, (compare Acts 7:2-4). The patriarch Terah then takes part of the family and starts the long journey to Canaan. However, their journey is interrupted for unknown reasons—perhaps Terah's health—and Abram's trip stalls in the city of Haran.

Personalize this lesson.

☑ When people unite in order to love, obey, and serve God, it is good! But sometimes people unite for purposes that do not honor God. What groups are you part of? Do your groups draw you closer to God? Or do they tempt you away from His purposes for you? How can you work in your relationships and groups to encourage yourself and the group to seek God more wholeheartedly? Ask God to show you something specific to say or do. Then look for an opportunity to do it this week.

Abram: Chosen, Chastised, and Choosing
Genesis 12–13

Memorize God's Word: Genesis 12:3.

❖ Genesis 12:1-3—Abram Called

1. When the Lord calls Abram, what three things does He command him to do?

   _____

   _____

   _____

2. What sevenfold promise does God make Abram?

   a. _____

   b. _____

   c. _____

   d. _____

   e. _____

   f. _____

   g. _____

3. What do you think Abram's obedience to God's command must have cost him? What did he gain?

   _____

   _____

   _____

❖ Genesis 12:4-9—Abram Obeying

4. How do you think Abram knew where to go when he left Haran? (See also Proverbs 3:5-6.)

_____

_____

5. What happens at his first stop, the oak of Moreh?

_____

_____

6. What happens at his next stop, the hills east of Bethel?

_____

_____

7. Abram's faith appears to be growing at this time. What do you think stimulated his faith?

_____

_____

_____

8. How does this understanding apply to the development of your own faith?

_____

_____

_____

❖ Genesis 12:10-20—Abram Stumbling

9. Why does Abram decide to leave Canaan?

_____

_____

10. How does he put his wife at risk to ensure his own safety?

_____

_____

11. How does the Lord intervene in this situation to rescue Abram and Sarai?

_____

_____

❖ Genesis 13:1-18—Abram Choosing

12. What suggests a renewal of Abram's faith following his trip to Egypt?

_____

_____

13. What problems arise that force Abram and Lot to separate?

_____

_____

14. Why does Lot choose to move to the plain of Jordan? How did this choice endanger Lot and his family?

_____

_____

_____

15. What does his willingness to let Lot choose tell us about Abram?

_____

_____

16. Why do you think God chose to speak to him at this time?

_____

_____

17. What principles control your decisions about your career and possessions? How do these issues relate to your spiritual life?

_____

_____

_____

❖ Genesis 12–13—Abram Blessed

18. What was required of Abram in his relationship with God? (See Hebrews 11:6.)

_____

_____

19. What is required of a person today who wants to know God? (See also John 5:24.)

_____

_____

20. How is such a qualification obtained? (See Ephesians 2:8-9.)

_____

_____

21. Who initiated the relationship between Abram and the Lord?

_____

_____

Apply what you have learned. What about your personal walk with God? Perhaps you have not yet started the journey, but here you are, attending a Bible study. Could it be that God is gently drawing you into a relationship with Himself? Abraham was called *"a friend of God"* (James 2:23) because in faith he chose to go God's way, not his own. We also can be called friends of God if we will step out in obedient faith (John 15:14), following Christ's way and not our own. If you haven't done so already, will you choose to start the journey today?

Abram: Chosen, Chastised, and Choosing
Genesis 12–13

Chapter 12 is the major turning point in the book of Genesis. Now God begins to bless all people through one man whose name initially was Abram. Without any notice, God calls Abram away from his home. He promises to bless him and all the nations of the world through his descendants. Though Abram begins hesitantly and fails periodically, he grows in his faith and obedience.

Chosen

God's first appearance to Abram takes place in Ur (Acts 7:2). Abram travels with Terah, his father, to Haran, where they stay for some time. After Terah dies Abram travels to the land of Canaan. In Genesis 12, Abram is in the early stages of his spiritual development; later he will come to a deep confidence in God. Genesis 12:1-3 records the Abrahamic Covenant, where God commands Abram to leave his home, and makes promises to him. Those promises are still being fulfilled. God made a great nation of Abram; and Muslims, Jews, and Christians highly regard his name. Most importantly, people have been blessed through the Lord Jesus Christ, Abraham's most notable descendant.

About 2085 BC, when Abram leaves Haran for Canaan, he is 75 years old; he brings his wife, Sarai, the family's possessions, and servants. Abram also brings his nephew Lot. Abram soon enters the land populated by Noah's grandson Canaan. Canaanite society's moral climate is terrible. Shortly after, *Yahweh* again appears to Abram, confirming His earlier promises. This story would be meaningful to the infant nation of Israel as they approached Canaan much later. They were not migrating to the Promised Land merely as a people looking for a homeland. They knew that God had designated the land for them many centuries before.

Chastised

Soon after Abram arrives in Canaan a severe famine causes him to move south, into Egypt. As they approach the Egyptian border, he realizes that Sarai's beauty might jeopardize him. The Egyptians would not hesitate to kill a man if they wanted his wife. Abram insists that Sarai pose as his sister, placing her in a terrible ethical dilemma. Abram may console himself with the fact that Sarai is his half sister, but deep inside he knows he is being deceptive. The couple finds conditions just as they have feared. Sarai is immediately conscripted to Pharaoh's harem, although it is likely that God protects her from committing adultery while in Pharaoh's house.

Think about obeying ungodly requests. Though our cultures are different, women today may face difficult decisions similar to Sarai's. There may be someone reading this who has been asked by a partner to participate in watching pornography, to experiment with drugs, or to share in illicit sex. Our decisions must always be based on God's Word. God protected Sarai because she was destined to play a leading role in the story of redemption, but there are no guarantees He will protect us when we make bad choices. We must obey God and His Word, even if we pay a price.

God protects the couple by afflicting the Egyptian king and members of his household with illness. Pharaoh traces the troubles back to the day he took Sarai. It is clear to him that Sarai is Abram's wife. This pagan king morally reproves Abram. For the moment, at least, Pharaoh's integrity seems to be superior to Abram's. Nevertheless, Pharaoh does not punish Abram, but sends him away wealthier than when he came.

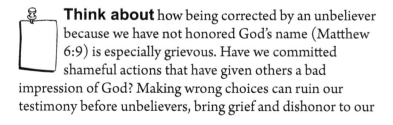

Think about how being corrected by an unbeliever because we have not honored God's name (Matthew 6:9) is especially grievous. Have we committed shameful actions that have given others a bad impression of God? Making wrong choices can ruin our testimony before unbelievers, bring grief and dishonor to our heavenly Father, and embarrass us. Our heart's desire must be to live in a way that honors and points people to the Lord.

God intends to protect His gracious plan of blessing the entire world through Abram and Sarai. Even though they jeopardize His intent by their deception, He is able to overcome the worst that men can do. Abram and Sarai also begin to learn that they dare not lean on their own cleverness in delivering themselves from dangerous situations. Trusting in the Lord is a more stable basis for safety than human brilliance. God intends for believers to use their own wits, but not to depend on them alone.

Choosing

Embarrassed but enriched, Abram returns to the Promised Land, arriving back at Bethel (*house of God*) where he had earlier camped. Abram's and Lot's herdsmen argue; they need to reach an agreement concerning sharing pasturelands and water sources. The honorable choice would be for the younger man to grant first choice to his older uncle. Abram, acting in the interests of *Yahweh's* reputation among the region's inhabitants, leaves the choice to Lot. Choosing the fertile plain and its water as his new home, Lot takes his portion of the family, his herds, and his flocks, and departs from his uncle. Abram will remain in Canaan's central highlands. Lot will live near the river, adjacent to Sodom, a town that would later become infamous for its immorality. Though the New Testament identifies Lot as a righteous believer (2 Peter 2:7-8), Sodom will affect Lot more than Lot affects Sodom.

Abram's actions in Genesis 13 establish the principle that the one who lives by faith is more concerned for God's reputation among the unconverted than for the increase of his own wealth. Significantly, it is only after Abram has made this critical choice that God again appears to Abram. He does so to reaffirm the promises He had made earlier. He challenges Abram to use the mountain on which he stands as a vantage point and to rejoice in the knowledge that all the land he could see from it would one day belong to him and to his offspring. The number of Abram's descendants would be staggering to contemplate. So Abram moves south and camps near Hebron, one of Canaan's principal southern cities. Again, he builds an altar and worships the Lord, leaving on the land a visible token of his devotion.

Personalize this lesson.

✓ Abraham was a worshiper. He worshiped in good times, when Sarai was safely returned to him, and in bad times, when Lot selfishly took the best pastureland for himself. It was second nature to him to express love and gratitude to God by offering his sacrifices. Because Christ died as the perfect sacrifice, animal sacrifice is no longer practiced, and New Testament Christians are no longer required to build an altar for such an offering. But having a special place in your home where you can go to fall on your knees and pray and worship is still a good idea. It might be in a closet, a seldom-used bedroom, or family room where you can close the door, ignore the phone, and have an intimate, private time with God. If you have small children, the moments may be short, but with the Lord's help those moments can become a cherished time that you look forward to with joyful expectation. You are going to meet the Lord of the universe!

Living in a Declining Society
Genesis 14

❖ **Genesis 14:1-16—The Dangers of Living in a Declining Society**

1. What are the names and the cities of the kings who join together to invade the Valley of Siddim?

2. What are the names and cities of the local kings who unite to defend themselves against the invaders?

3. What prompts the invasion?

4. Why is the outcome of the battle so significant for Abram?

5. What action does Abram take when he learns of Lot's capture?

6. What are at least four things we can learn about Abram from verses 13-16?

   _____

   _____

7. Why would Abram have been justified in not getting involved in Lot's trouble?

   _____

   _____

8. Can you recall and share a time when God rescued you from a difficult or dangerous situation of your own making?

   _____

   _____

❖ Genesis 14:17-20—Abram's Meeting With the King of Salem

NOTE: Melchizedek, King of *Salem* (later called Jerusalem) is a mysterious figure mentioned in Scripture in Genesis 14, Psalm 110, and finally in Hebrews 7 as a *foreshadowing* or *picture of Christ*.

9. What information does each of these passages give us about Melchizedek?

   a. Genesis 14:17-20 _____

   _____

   b. Psalm 110:1-4 _____

   _____

   c. Hebrews 7:1-5 _____

   _____

10. What does Melchizedek bring to Abram when they meet in the Valley of Kings?

   _____

   _____

11. How was this symbolic of the Cross of the Lord Jesus Christ (Luke 22:14-20)?

_____

_____

_____

12. What significant gift does Melchizedek bestow on Abram at this time?

_____

_____

13. This gift helped Abram put his victory in proper perspective. Why was this important?

_____

_____

14. What does Abram, in return, give to Melchizedek? What is the significance of this?

_____

_____

_____

15. What does Hebrews 7:24-28 tell us about the priestly work of Christ on our behalf?

_____

_____

_____

❖ Genesis 14:21-24—Abram's Rejection of the King of Sodom

16. What can we conclude about the King of Sodom from Genesis 13:13; 18:20-21; and 19:1-13?

_____

_____

17. Why do you think he offers to give Abram the spoils of victory?

_____

_____

18. Why does Abram refuse his offer of riches?

_____

_____

19. What does this tell us about Abram? (See also Hebrews 11:8-10; Psalm 24:1.)

_____

_____

20. Has there been a time in your life when you had to choose between the riches of the world and the things of God? Will you share what influenced your choice?

_____

_____

_____

Apply what you have learned. Abram is a smart, strategic thinker—but rather than depending on his selfish cleverness as he'd done in Egypt (Lesson 6)—here he devises a brilliant military move to rescue his nephew Lot, even though Lot has treated his uncle selfishly. Again he uses strategic thinking in refusing riches from the king of Sodom. Never would that king be able to come back and claim any right to rule over Abram and his household. What has made the difference? Faith in *"the LORD, God Most High, Possessor of heaven and earth"* (Genesis 14:22) is enabling Abram to use his mental sharpness and his resources in a godly way. Trusting God fully can do the same for us. In fact, that's the smartest strategic move we can make!

Living in a Declining Society
Genesis 14

Lot separates from Abram and exchanges a place of blessing for life in a wicked society. Abram's decision to trust God to provide for him is confirmed. By contrast, Lot is captured in the fall of Sodom and its sister cities. Abram risks his life to save Lot and declares the sufficiency of *Yahweh*, God Most High, before Sodom's king. Abram shows strength of character and God-honoring faith.

The leading king of the region was Chedorlaomer of Elam. The small cities aligned with such leaders sent them funds every year, to secure the king's assistance if their thrones or their cities were threatened. The kings of the five city-states of the lower Jordan valley finally rebel against Chedorlaomer, whose allies are willing to fight because of the potential plunder. After a year of preparation, the armies move south. Once underway, the invaders prove invincible. Lot's family and possessions are considered part of the invaders' plunder of Sodom. Lot probably expects to spend the rest of his life as a slave.

Think about grace. Lot's selfish choices put him in a serious predicament. In choosing the best pastureland he showed utter disrespect for his uncle. When an escaped captive came to tell Abram about his nephew's capture, Abram went immediately to help Lot. Abram, who was not young, could have refused, but God was transforming his character. Grace is getting what you don't deserve. When Abram acted in grace toward Lot, God acted in grace toward him. He gave him victory in battle although he was greatly outnumbered.

The Duties Toward a Declining Society

Along the journey north, one of the captives escapes. He finds Abram near Hebron and reports his nephew's capture. In verse 13, for the first time in the Bible, Abram is called *"Abram the Hebrew."* Abram felt a responsibility to rescue his nephew from the invading kings. He was able to call on 318 trained men born in his household, his servants' offspring.

Some argue that 318 men would not be able to defeat the armies of four battle-hardened northern kings, but the text does not say that Abram's soldiers take on the entire armies. Abram and his friends likely pursue a slow-moving portion of the larger force—consisting of women, children, the elderly, and plunder—and catch up with them near Dan, at Canaan's northern extremity. Abram and his men hike over 125 miles, probably with little rest, and attack the northern army at night. Abram's companions continue the attack against the raiders for another 50 miles. Along the way, they recover all the people and possessions taken from Sodom. Again, Abram proves to be a blessing—not only to Lot and his family, but to all the captives.

The Testimony of Faith Before a Declining Society

The people of Sodom and their king meet the triumphant Abram upon his return. Then we meet Melchizedek, king of Salem. The contrasts between the king of Sodom and the king of Salem are significant. The king of Sodom comes to improve his political position. The king of Salem comes to bless Abram. The king of Sodom falsely poses as Abram's generous-hearted benefactor. The king of Salem brings gifts to sustain and bless the weary but victorious Patriarch.

In the entire Old Testament, only this passage and Psalm 110:4 refer to Melchizedek. In the New Testament, Hebrews 7 reveals him as a highly important person. He and Abram both worship *Yahweh.* Melchizedek, whose name means *king of righteousness*, is both a king and a priest. He serves as a type of Jesus Christ and arrives with no fanfare. Even the omissions in the account are highly significant. Melchizedek appears *"without father or mother or genealogy, having neither beginning of days nor end of life, but resembling the Son of God he continues a priest forever"* (Hebrews 7:3). Jesus is declared to be a High Priest according to Melchizedek's order (Psalm 110:4). It is also significant that Melchizedek brings bread and wine symbolizing Christ's death on the cross (1 Corinthians 11:23-26). Melchizedek sees God's hand in Abram's victory. Abram offers to the great priest a 10ᵗʰ of the battle's spoils, acknowledging that God is the true Source of all his blessings.

The king of Sodom comes to him posing as a benefactor, wanting to appear before Abram and the people of Sodom as a liberator rather than the coward he is. He "generously" suggests to Abram that the Patriarch keep the possessions gained in the battle. The king wants only the citizens of Sodom to return home with him.

Think about benefiting from an unholy alliance. Given the opportunity to profit as richly as Abram would have by receiving the plunder from his victory, could you have resisted? He won the battle and earned the reward. Abram believed that to capitalize from the victory would tarnish his reputation and weaken his testimony to his pagan neighbors. The New Testament warns us against forming alliances with unbelievers, no matter how profitable they might be. *"Do not be unequally yoked with unbelievers. For what partnership has righteousness with lawlessness? Or what fellowship has light with darkness?"* (2 Corinthians 6:14). Whether the partnership is a business or personal alliance, we must be careful. How we make money can affect our reputation and our witness to the unbelieving world. Money itself is not evil; it's the love of it that gets us in trouble. Before the temptation ever occurs, spend time with the Lord and settle the question.

Abram is too wise to yield to the king's tactic. He had previously sworn that he would not allow the king to enrich him. That wicked king will never be able to go before the world and announce that he has made Abram rich. Abram depends solely on *Yahweh*. The only "wages" he will accept are the modest amounts of food consumed by his trained force. The Gentiles who ally themselves with Abram are blessed, and Abram maintains his testimony before the pagans living in the Promised Land.

Personalize this lesson.

Genesis 14 is a picture of a battle well-fought, and we can learn from it. We will probably never go to war with the likes of King Chedorlaomer. But whether we realize it or not, we all do battle with "rulers" on a daily basis. We are in a spiritual battle. Paul wrote, *"We do not wrestle against flesh and blood, but against the rulers, against the authorities, against the cosmic powers over this present darkness, against the spiritual forces of evil in the heavenly places"* (Ephesians 6:12). To be prepared, we need to know what our resources are and how to use them. God will go into battle with us as He did with Abram, and in His strength, we will win. But we must obey His commands—and we must pray! How might you, through prayer, do battle on behalf of those in spiritual captivity? *"Be strong in the Lord and in the strength of His might"* (Ephesians 6:10).

Trusting God's Promises
Genesis 15–16

Memorize God's Word: Genesis 15:6.

❖ Genesis 15:1-6—Abram Believes God's Promise

1. What does God promise Abram (Genesis 15:1)?

   _____

   _____

2. In light of events described in Genesis 14, what concerns or fears was Abram facing?

   _____

   _____

3. What concerns or fears are you facing today?

   _____

   _____

4. How does God's promise to Abram in Genesis 15:1 relate to his concerns and yours?

   _____

   _____

5. Abram expresses a great concern in verse 2. What solution did he envision?

   _____

   _____

6. Does God's response indicate that He was displeased or offended by Abram's question? How does He address Abram's very real and great concern?

_____

_____

7. On what basis did Abram believe God's promise of a son from his own body? (See Romans 4:18-22.)

_____

_____

8. According to Genesis 15:6, how did God respond to Abram's faith?

_____

_____

❖ Genesis 15:7-21—God's Covenant With Abram

9. a. Describe the covenant recorded here. Include who made this covenant and who keeps it.

      _____

      _____

  b. What ceremony confirmed it? _____

      _____

      _____

10. Why is the fact that Abram was sleeping when the covenant was ratified significant?

_____

_____

11. At what point in history did God initially fulfill this covenant? (See Joshua 1:1-5; 21:43-45.)

_____

_____

12. What additional prophetic information concerning the future of his descendants (Israel) did God give Abram at this time?

    _____

    _____

13. When and how was this prophecy fulfilled in history? (See Exodus 1:1-14; 3:1-10; 9:13-14; 12:31-42.)

    _____

    _____

14. Why do you think God delayed the fulfillment of His promise concerning the land for such a long time?

    _____

    _____

15. The covenant in this passage relates specifically to the nation of Israel. What promise about Jesus is the church still waiting for God to fulfill? (See Acts 1:9-11.)

    _____

    _____

16. Why has God delayed the fulfillment of this promise? (See 2 Peter 3:8-9.)

    _____

    _____

❖ Genesis 16—The Faltering Faith of the Chosen

17. What very specific promise had God given Abram in Genesis 15:4?

    _____

    _____

18. Why do you think Abram and Sarai decided to take matters into their own hands?

    _____

    _____

19. What culturally accepted solution to their problem does Sarai propose? What should they have done instead?

_____

_____

20. What were the immediate and long-term consequences of their decision?

_____

_____

21. Describe Hagar's encounter with God, and tell what she learned about Him from this experience.

_____

_____

_____

Apply what you have learned. In chapters 15–16, the main character is not Abram, but God. Notice how strongly His presence is portrayed in chapter 15: He is the Rewarder of faithfulness (15:1, 6). He is the God of hope and promises (15:4-5, 7). He gives reassurance (15:8-19). He knows the future (15:13-14). He shows Himself trustworthy. Now notice His absence at the beginning of chapter 16. Abram and Sarai talk about God, but do not pray. They choose to solve the baby dilemma in a very human, but ungodly, way. The results are hatred and contention. When we leave God out and choose not to trust Him, the results are the same for us. Notice one final thing: God's mercy reaches out to a maidservant, enabling her to trust Him and face a difficult situation. How different the story would have been if only Abram and Sarai had trusted God. What steps of faith can you take to avoid the "if onlys" in your life?

Trusting God's Promises
Genesis 15–16

God's generosity is easily seen in these two chapters: God makes or confirms promises of future kindness. He then proves His intentions by appearing personally to Abram. Sarai and Abram's attempt to accelerate God's plan backfires. Here Scripture drives home the need for patient hope for those who await God's rewards.

The Promise of Abundant Offspring

God appears to Abram in a vision, bringing him *"the word of the LORD"* (15:1). This marks the first use of this expression in the Bible. It appears again in verse 4 and suggests the importance of the promise God is about to make. Abram is not to fear, but to trust in the One who has already proved to be his shield and will be his reward. Abram unburdens his heart to God and approaches Him with unusual reverence and submission. His childless condition weighs heavily on him. Though he possesses great wealth and supervises an enormous household, he lacks an heir. His name means *exalted father,* but he is not a father at all. Were he to die, his servant Eliezer would inherit all his wealth.

Think about God's comforting presence. Many believers say that the Lord makes His presence most felt during times of great testing. Abram was in distress. He recognized that, humanly speaking, it would take a miracle to have an heir. The Scripture says, *"No unbelief made him waver"* (Romans 4:20), but it does not say there was no tension, no battle going on, as he struggled to hold on to his faith. He was open and honest with God. He asked Him how He was going to solve this. Then the *"the word*

of the LORD" came to Abram in a vision. Trust Him to speak
through His Word when you are being tested. He will do it.

In the vision, God says Abram's heir will not be a servant, but his own
flesh-and-blood son. Abram's descendants will be so numerous that they
will resemble the stars of the night sky. Abram believes what God has
said, and Moses notes that Yahweh *"counted it to him as righteousness"*
(Genesis 15:6). The New Testament quotes or alludes to this verse many
times. God declares him righteous, though Abram remains a sinner who
will stumble many times.

The Promise Confirmed by Covenant

God reaffirms His earlier promise of title to the land of Canaan and
confirms His Word by issuing a covenant. Sometimes the parties to
a covenant pictured the bitter consequences of betrayal by walking
together between pieces of slaughtered animals to suggest, "May the
one who breaks this agreement suffer the fate of these creatures." God
instructs Abram to fetch *"a heifer three years old, a female goat three years
old, a ram three years old, a turtledove, and a young pigeon"* (15:9). Abram
cuts them in two and arranges them opposite each other, creating a
pathway down the center of the paired pieces.

Abram falls into a divinely imposed sleep, but one that is agitated by
a *"dreadful and great darkness"* (15:12), suggesting that the path to the
Promised Land would be long and painful. Abram has asked for sure
knowledge, and God provides it: *"Know for certain ... "* (15:13). God
lists four certainties: (1) Abram's descendants will live as strangers in
a distant land; (2) they will be enslaved and mistreated; (3) their exile
and bondage will last for four centuries; (4) they will return to the
Promised Land and possess it. In the darkness, Abram watches as *"a
smoking fire pot and a flaming torch passed between these pieces"* (15:17) of
the slaughtered animals. The two fiery items represent God's zeal and His
unapproachable purity. God is assuming all responsibility for fulfilling the
covenant, which includes the possession of the land by Abram's offspring.

The Attempt to Hasten the Promise Fails

Sarai is barren. Learning of God's renewed promise to give Abram a son
from his own body, she suggests that they use a practice common in the

ancient Near East: A barren wife could legally obtain offspring by using a surrogate. Sarai urges Abram, *"Go in to my servant; it may be that I shall obtain children by her"* (16:2). But this plan is born of convenience, not faith. Abram and Sarai are past the natural childbearing age, and Sarai dismisses God's promise to give them a supernatural conception. Their meddling produces a long string of human miseries.

Abram agrees to Sarai's proposal, and soon Hagar, the maidservant, is pregnant. Sarai now blames Abram for the consequences of her own idea. After harsh treatment from Sarai, Hagar flees into the wilderness. She heads for Egypt, moving west into the northern Sinai. There the Angel of the LORD, a person who appears here in Scripture for the first time, finds her. The Angel speaks with divine authority that Hagar recognizes and to which she submits. Bible scholars generally recognize the Angel of the LORD as an early appearance of Jesus Christ, the second person of the Trinity. Proof of this is the Angel's ceasing to appear in Scripture after Jesus enters the world in human flesh.

Hagar learns that God has not ignored her plight. Though she has been a victim of Sarai's scheme to hasten the fulfillment of God's promise, she bears the Patriarch's child. God directs her to return to Sarai. He will make her a mother to large numbers of offspring. The Angel predicts that she will bear a son, to be named *Ishmael* (*God hears*) to remind her of the prayers she uttered out of her misery.

Think about how much God cares. Abram and Melchizedek called God *El Elyon*—*"God Most High"* (14:18, 22). But Hagar called Him *El Roi*—*the God who sees me* (16:13-14)—because He came to her in the wilderness. When she was feeling very much alone and uncared for, God saw and He came. What an encouragement it would be if we realized that God sees our pain and cares. First Peter 5:7 urges each of us to cast all our cares and anxiety on Him, *"because He cares for you."*

Personalize this lesson.

☑ David wrote Psalm 37 to encourage God's people to trust Him even when He doesn't act on their time schedule. Verse 7 says, *"Be still before the LORD and wait patiently for Him."* Abram was a relatively new believer in the Lord God, and he allowed himself to be influenced by current customs in his pagan society. He made a bad choice—one that brought him heartache as long as he lived. The hostility between the descendants of Abram's firstborn son Ishmael, the Arabs, and those of Isaac, the Jews, has continued to this day.

Nobody ever said waiting is easy. Our restless society wants instant gratification. No wonder it's so hard for us to wait on the Lord. So when our schedules and the Lord's don't match, remember, He is the One who is sovereign, and no amount of fretting on our part will change His timetable. Praying is recommended as we wait—pray for His intervention, pray for peace. It's possible that we—and perhaps our descendants—may spend a lifetime regretting it if we run out of patience and take matters into our own hands. What important decision are you involved with right now? How can you invite God into that process?

The Sign of God's Covenant With Abraham
Genesis 17

❖ Genesis 17:1-8—Confirmation of the Covenant

1. How many years have passed since God first promised to make Abram's descendants into a great nation? (See Genesis 12:1-4.)

   _____

2. What seemingly insurmountable problems are involved in the fulfillment of this promise? (See Genesis 11:30; 17:17.)

   _____

   _____

   _____

3. What are long-term results from the way Abram and Sarai attempted to resolve this difficulty themselves? (See Genesis 16.)

   _____

   _____

4. What is the purpose of the Lord's appearance to Abram at this time?

   _____

   _____

5. What two commands does God give Abram in these verses?

   _____

   _____

   _____

6. What do you think these commands mean?

    _____

    _____

7. Using a dictionary or a Bible dictionary, explain the term
    covenant.

    _____

    _____

8. In this passage, who is making a covenant, and what does it
    include?

    _____

    _____

9. What is the meaning of Abram's new name, Abraham? Why
    does God change Abram's name at this time?

    _____

    _____

10. What name does God call Himself in this passage? How does
    this name guarantee His ability to keep His promises?

    _____

    _____

❖ Genesis 17:9-14—Abraham's Responsibilities in the Covenant

11. What would Abraham and his descendants have to do as a sign
    of their participation in this covenant?

    _____

    _____

12. What penalty would those who failed to observe this obligation
    face?

    _____

    _____

13. What spiritual symbolism did God intend this covenant to have? (See also Romans 2:28-29.)

_____

_____

14. With the covenant and its obligations, God was setting apart a people who would be His very own. What must we do today to be included in God's family? (See John 1:12; Galatians 3:6-9.)

_____

_____

_____

15. What is the wonderfully reassuring "seal" of the covenant that God has made with us? (See Ephesians 1:13.)

_____

_____

❖ Genesis 17:15-22—Sarai's Inclusion in the Covenant

16. What specific promise does God make in this passage regarding Sarah?

_____

_____

17. Considering how Abraham first reacts (17:17), what does this tell you about faith?

_____

_____

_____

18. Which of God's promises are difficult for you to believe? How does God want you to respond to these "hard-to-believe" promises?

_____

_____

19. What indication do we have in this passage that Abraham is still depending on Ishmael as the means through which God will fulfill the covenant?

_____

_____

20. What other reasons do you think Abraham might have had for asking God to bless Ishmael?

_____

_____

❖ Genesis 17:23-27—Abraham's Obedience to the Covenant

21. How is Abraham's response to God in these verses an example for us to follow?

_____

_____

22. Re-read Genesis 17. What are at least four important attributes of God illustrated in this chapter?

_____

_____

Apply what you have learned. Don't you love the part of the story where Abraham falls down laughing and talks to himself? God has already planned magnificently for both him and his wife! The fact that Sarah's conceiving is so humanly impossible that it is laughable doesn't even enter into the discussion. Or that Ishmael is a living, breathing result of a lack of trust. God is committed to Abraham. God is no less committed to us! As soon as the Lord finished speaking to him, Abraham got up and acted in faith and obedience. What "impossible" promises of God will you claim in faith?

The Sign of God's Covenant With Abraham
Genesis 17

After Ishmael's birth, 13 long years pass while Abram and Sarai grow older. The biblical account records no communication from God; He has become silent, leaving the couple to remember His past promises. Abram is 99 and Sarai is 89, both well past childbearing age. When hope is faint, God appears to Abram to confirm His earlier promises. This time God becomes specific: A son will be born to the chosen family within a year. In preparation, the couple is given new and meaningful names. The newly renamed Abraham is to testify to his confidence in God by circumcising himself and the males of his household.

God Renews His Covenant

For over a decade, *Yahweh* has not made Himself known to the chosen family, but finally Abram sees Him. Abram will have a son, and the promised heir will come from Sarai's womb. Abram's responsibility is to *"walk before* [Him], *and be blameless"* (17:1). God is calling on Abraham to live a life that will pass God's inspection, a standard considerably higher than man's. Godly believers are always conscious that God is watching. *Blameless* in this context does not mean *sinless* but *lacking an obvious fault*. In the Job stories, the noun form of the word *blameless* may appear as *integrity* (Job 27:5). Abraham is to walk before God in a consistently blameless way, even in the areas that only God sees.

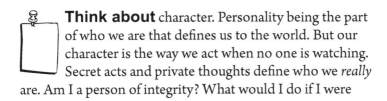 **Think about** character. Personality being the part of who we are that defines us to the world. But our character is the way we act when no one is watching. Secret acts and private thoughts define who we *really* are. Am I a person of integrity? What would I do if I were

given change for a $50 bill instead of a $5 bill and had walked
out of the store in a strange town before I discovered it?
Would the thought that no one would ever know cross my
mind? *Blameless* and *integrity* are used interchangeably in
Scripture. In this context, integrity means *unimpaired moral
principles*. Character matters. It reflects on our Father when
the world sees our obvious faults, and our hidden faults
reflect our character to the God who sees all.

Abram falls facedown in submission. If he'd had any thoughts that God
had abandoned him, they were now answered. His name will now be
Abraham—the father of Israel and also of many nations. God adds a
new pledge: Kings will be among Abraham's offspring. God's generous
promises can be summarized under two headings: Abraham will have
great numbers of children, and God will be faithful to Abraham and
those children forever. As a pledge of His covenant, God ensures that the
very land where Abraham camps as an alien will one day belong to his
descendants.

Abraham must keep God's covenant and be a role model. God calls for
Abraham and his male offspring to undergo circumcision as a *"sign of
the covenant"* (17:11). Future generations will submit to it on the eighth
day after they are born, designating them as holy and members of the
covenant family. It did not guarantee them righteous standing before
God, who views neglect of this rite as a crime. The offender *"shall be cut
off from his people"* (17:14). It was intended to express union with the
community, but later generations wrongly saw it as the sole condition of
righteous standing with God.

In Genesis 17:15 we see that Sarai will now be known as *Sarah*, meaning,
simply, *princess*. It is highly significant. Hagar, and perhaps others, had
despised Sarah for her failure to produce an heir. Now she will become a
princess to the world at large, as she becomes the mother of nations and
kings. Sarah is the only woman in the Bible whose name is changed and
whose age at death is stated.

Think about God's patience. Sarah was miraculously protected in Pharaoh's harem, and now, well past childbearing age, she is supernaturally enabled to conceive a child. She is imperfect. She encourages Abraham to follow custom and obtain an heir through Hagar rather than waiting for God to fulfill His promise. She then complains bitterly to him because he does what she suggests. At times she seems unstable and other times merely irritable, but God never gives up on her. God looks beyond her failings with a higher calling—*"mother of nations"* (17:16, NIV). God does not give up on us, either. He has a high calling in Christ for us as well. God is patient, but we must not try His patience. Let's cooperate fully in the work He has begun in our lives.

At the staggering promise he has just heard, the Patriarch again falls on his face with an outburst of laughter—a mixture of joy, amazement, and at least a degree of disbelief: *"Shall a child be born to a man who is a hundred years old?"* (17:17). Abraham's unbelief seems to be mild and secondary. His main concern is Ishmael, now about 13 years old. Rather than reacting with total joy at the long-delayed prospect of a son through Sarah, he expresses an intense wish that Ishmael might be the promised heir. The son to be born will be named *Isaac*, Hebrew for *he laughs*, or *he will laugh*. God will have the last laugh, and Sarah's skepticism will be turned to joy.

God will not abandon or neglect Ishmael; he will become the father of many children. Twelve rulers will come from him, and he will become known as a patriarch himself. Yet he will remain outside the terms of the Abrahamic covenant. Those blessings will be reserved for Isaac and his offspring. On the same day the promise is delivered, Abraham circumcises all the male members of his household, beginning with himself. Once God's expectations are clear, the best time to obey is always immediately.

Personalize this lesson.

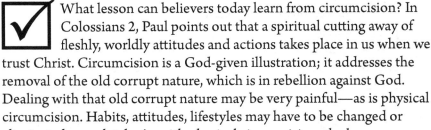 What lesson can believers today learn from circumcision? In Colossians 2, Paul points out that a spiritual cutting away of fleshly, worldly attitudes and actions takes place in us when we trust Christ. Circumcision is a God-given illustration; it addresses the removal of the old corrupt nature, which is in rebellion against God. Dealing with that old corrupt nature may be very painful—as is physical circumcision. Habits, attitudes, lifestyles may have to be changed or eliminated completely. As with physical circumcision, the longer we wait, the more painful the surgery. If God tells us to stop doing something, to change our behavior—or our thinking—the sooner we do it, the better off we will be.

Some of us need to change our entire lifestyle. For others, a long, stubbornly held view must be honestly re-examined. If God convicts us of bad habits, a bad attitude, or unacceptable behavior, then it has to go! Products of that old corrupt nature must be cut away. Our hearts must be circumcised. God expects obedience, and He has offered to help us. What part of your life is uncircumcised?

Abraham the Intercessor
Genesis 18

Memorize God's Word: Genesis 18:14a.

❖ Genesis 18:1-15—A Visit From God

1. How would you describe the scene of God's next appearance to Abraham (18:1-2)?

   _____

   _____

2. What clues to the visitors' identity does the text give? (See also Genesis 18:25; 19:1.)

   _____

   _____

3. What is Abraham's immediate response to his unexpected visitors?

   _____

   _____

4. Do you think Abraham knew who these exalted visitors were? Why or why not?

   _____

   _____

5. What important announcement does the Lord make at this time?

   _____

6. Why was it important for Sarah to hear God's announcement for herself? (See also Romans 10:14, 17.)

_____

_____

7. How does she react, and why?

_____

_____

8. How did Abraham react to a similar message from God? (See Genesis 17:15-17.)

_____

_____

9. What can we learn about a life of faith from their reactions?

_____

_____

_____

10. How do we know that Sarah believed God's promise, even though it sounded impossible? (See Hebrews 11:11 in the English Standard Version, New King James Version, or New American Standard Bible.)

_____

_____

11. On what did she base her faith?

_____

_____

12. Compare Genesis 16:1-2, 5 and 18:12-15 with 1 Peter 3:5-6. What events from Sarah's life are missing from the 1 Peter passage? Why might the Holy Spirit have led Peter to omit these events?

_____

_____

❖ Genesis 18:16-21—A Disclosure From God

13. According to this passage, why did God choose to tell Abraham what He was about to do in Sodom and Gomorrah?

    _____

    _____

14. What else does James 2:23 tell us about God's relationship with Abraham?

    _____

    _____

15. What bearing would this have had on God's decision to tell Abraham what He was about to do? (See John 15:14-15.)

    _____

    _____

❖ Genesis 18:22-33—Intercessor Before God

16. Who was Abraham thinking of when he interceded for the *"righteous people"* in Sodom?

    _____

    _____

17. On what basis did he make his requests?

    _____

    _____

18. What was God's response to Abraham's intercession?

    _____

    _____

19. What can we learn about intercessory prayer from the following passages?

    a.   Daniel 9:18_____

    _____

    b. John 16:26-27 _____

_____

    c. Ephesians 6:18 _____

_____

    d. James 5:16 _____

_____

20. What attribute of God do you see in this chapter that is especially meaningful to you, and why?

_____

_____

_____

_____

Apply what you have learned. Sometimes we forget that prayer is not just our talking to God, but also God talking to us. If we're talking more than 50 percent of the time, then we're hogging the conversation! Note what the Lord said to Abraham about Sarah's silent laughter and doubting thoughts: *"Is anything too hard for the LORD?"* (Genesis 18:14). At the moment when Sarah should have been listening intently to the Lord because of the wonderful promise He was making, she was focusing on herself. Then she made matters worse by jumping in with a lie, claiming that she had not laughed. How ridiculous—to lie to God, as if He didn't know. Learn from Sarah's mistakes: Listen when you pray! God can show you who He is (in this case, omnipotent), and what He either has done or will do for you, as you read the promises in His Word.

Abraham the Intercessor
Genesis 18

When Yahweh first calls Abraham, He tells him that he will be blessed and should be a blessing in return. Genesis 18 provides an excellent example of this. When God plans to destroy the cities of Sodom and Gomorrah because of their wickedness, Abraham becomes a blessing to the people of those towns by interceding for them.

God Reaffirms His Blessing of Abraham

God appears to Abraham fewer than a dozen times over the course of Abraham's 175-year lifespan. As Genesis 18 opens, He again visits Abraham, who is living near Hebron. At first Abraham seems not to recognize the Lord, who appears as a man accompanied by two other men. Abraham regards his visitors as distinguished individuals at the very least and begs for the privilege of showing them his best hospitality. A choice calf is prepared. Sarah bakes fresh bread. Though Abraham is head of a sizable clan and an important man, he serves as the waiter.

The guests inquire about Sarah by name, convincing Abraham that he is entertaining divine representatives. *Yahweh* reveals Himself in His statement in 18:10, *"I will surely return to you about this time next year, and Sarah your wife shall have a son."* (The two who accompany Him are identified as angels in 19:1.) When Sarah, who is eavesdropping on the conversation, hears that she is to bear a son—a physical impossibility for a post-menopausal woman—she laughs to herself in unbelief. Yet God has been faithful to every statement He has made in her life already. Why should she doubt Him now? God finds her laughter offensive, and says so to Abraham.

Sarah then compounds the blunder by denying she laughed. The Lord does not let her denial go unchallenged; He rebukes her. God asks whether anything is too *"hard"* for Him, reminding Abraham that His power is limitless, and that, regardless of Sarah's laughter, He will bless Abraham with a son the following year.

Abraham Intercedes to Bless Others

Only a short distance east of Hebron is the Dead Sea, with the communities of Sodom and Gomorrah. As Abraham's visitors begin to walk east, he walks with them toward the valley. God uses this intimate situation to reveal a grave matter to the Patriarch. Many people have been complaining, either in prayer or otherwise, about the horrible situation in the two towns. God refuses to judge the towns simply because of those complaints; He is determined to discover firsthand their exact moral condition. If the complaints are true, Sodom and Gomorrah will be destroyed.

Think about your view of God. God is omnipotent, omnipresent, and omniscient; that is, all-powerful, present everywhere, and all-knowing. Therefore, we can assume He knew exactly how great the sin of Sodom and Gomorrah was before He "went down" to investigate. Why did He conduct this investigation? To demonstrate His justice; to reveal to Abraham that He would not take action that violated His character. It was important to God that the man He had chosen to bless *"all the families of the earth"* have a correct concept of God as both loving and just. We, also, need to understand this aspect of God's character in order to accept some of the "harsh realities" of life in a fallen world.

At this point Abraham becomes an intercessor. Genesis 18:22 points out, *"Abraham still stood before the LORD."* To *stand before* someone, in the Hebrew Bible, often suggests service in prayer. The Patriarch is about to save lives by praying for people, a ministry that every believer in Jesus Christ is called to join (1 Timothy 2:1). When we intercede, we imitate the Lord Jesus Himself, who hung on the cross and prayed, *"Father, forgive them, for they know not what they do"* (Luke 23:34).

Abraham has a personal interest in Sodom, because his nephew Lot and

Lot's family live there. In spite of the troubles between their herdsmen, he loves his nephew. Abraham knows that whatever Lot's failings are, he is a true worshiper of *Yahweh* and a man who is grieved by his neighbors' godless behavior (2 Peter 2:7-8).

Abraham begins to pray for Lot—and for any others who might be properly described as righteous. In doing so, he becomes a blessing to Lot and his family, and might have been—had there been other righteous people—a blessing to others as well. Praying for others is an important way that God's people can spread His blessings upon those around them.

Intercession—the pleading of a believer for the welfare of others— builds upon sound doctrine, and it is so in Abraham's prayer. Knowing *Yahweh* as he does, it is unthinkable that the righteous *"Judge of all the earth"* should open Himself to the charge of injustice in His dealings with humanity. Abraham understood that to *"sweep away the righteous with the wicked"* is inconsistent with God's character. Abraham suggests that Sodom might contain as many as 50 righteous people. God acknowledges that, should 50 righteous people live there, He would not destroy the place. Encouraged by this, Abraham asks whether even smaller numbers of righteous people might allow the city to be saved. In each case, God agrees to spare the city for the sake of the righteous. Satisfied that God will do what is right, Abraham returns to Mamre. Eventually, not even 10 righteous are found, but God spares Lot and his family by evacuating them from the city (19:15-16).

Personalize this lesson.

☑ Genesis is the book of beginnings, and what we see in chapter 18 is the first instance of intercessory prayer. Intercessors must approach God as Abraham did, with reverence, boldness, and persistence. We can intercede with the expectation that God will answer if we ask according to His will. Our source for knowing that is His written Word. Nations, governments, and countless people desperately need us to intercede for them before the throne of God. Let Abraham's example encourage us to do so. William Temple wrote, "When I pray, coincidences happen, and when I don't pray, they don't." What efforts are you willing to make in order to make *coincidences* happen in your life and the lives of your neighbors? Who needs your intercession this week?

Lesson 12

Corruption Judged and Destroyed
Genesis 19

❖ Genesis 19:1-11—Depravity: The Sodomites Reveal Their Wickedness

1. When does Lot become aware of the visitors' true identity?

   _____

   _____

2. a. What initial effort does Lot make to ensure their safety and welfare?

   _____

   _____

   b. Why does he do this?

   _____

   _____

3. How are the Sodomites' true feelings about Lot revealed in this passage?

   _____

   _____

4. Why do you think they had tolerated Lot until this time? (See Genesis 14.)

   _____

   _____

   _____

5. What evils in our own society also merit God's judgment even if they are legal and the majority of people accept them?

_____

_____

_____

6. According to Jesus (Matthew 10:14-15 and Luke 10:8-12), what sin against God deserves even greater judgment than Sodom's evils?

_____

_____

❖ Genesis 19:12-22—Deliverance: God Demonstrates His Ability to Rescue

7. Why did God rescue Lot from the destruction of Sodom? (See Genesis 19:29 and 2 Peter 2:5-9.)

_____

_____

8. What assurance and encouragement does this give you?

_____

_____

_____

9. Even though 2 Peter 2:5-9 says Lot was righteous, give an example of how ineffective his influence was on the people around him.

_____

_____

10. What actions or attitudes could have caused him to lose credibility even with his own family?

_____

_____

❖ Genesis 19:23-29—Destruction: Abraham Witnesses God's Judgment on the Cities

11. How would you describe the scope of God's judgment on the cities and surrounding plains?

12. Why do you think His judgment was so extensive?

13. Why do you think Lot's wife looked back?

14. What warning does Jesus say we should draw from her fate? (See Luke 17:30-33)

15. What do you think Jesus meant by this warning?

❖ Genesis 19:30-38—Decadence: Lot and His Daughters

16. Given their primary concern for descendants, how did Lot's daughters choose to solve their problem?

17. Do you think their concern was justified? Why or why not?

18. What two nations descended from the immorally conceived offspring of Lot's daughters? What do Deuteronomy 23:3-6 and Zephaniah 2:9-10 tell us about these nations?

_____

_____

_____

19. Remember Lot's reason for settling among the Sodomites. (See Genesis 13:10-13.) What did Lot and his family gain when they moved to Sodom? What did they lose?

_____

_____

_____

_____

Apply what you have learned. Who was to blame for the actions of Lot's daughters as they sought to preserve their family line? The young women were only acting in line with the culture of Sodom, where they were reared. These daughters had neither godly influences nor godly examples to instruct them. Consider how they might have been different if their family had spent time with Uncle Abraham and Aunt Sarah during their early years, instead of in Sin City. The apostle Paul wrote to his spiritual children in Corinth, *"I became your father in Christ Jesus through the gospel. I urge you, then, be imitators of me"* (1 Corinthians 4:15-16). Let's learn from Lot what not to do. Rather, let's be sure our children live surrounded by godly influences, especially as they observe in us a Christ-like life worth imitating. What young people are you modeling Christ to?

Corruption Judged and Destroyed
Genesis 19

Genesis 18 and 19 are written in parallel form to show the contrast between Abraham and his morally compromised nephew, Lot. Abraham entertains angels at his home in the country and Lot entertains them at his house in an evil city. Lot becomes a picture of the believer who permits wickedness to obtain a foothold in his life. He is a strange mixture of moral outrage and personal weakness. In spite of him, rather than because of him, God answers Abraham's prayer for justice.

Depravity: Wickedness Revealed

Lot's sad story begins with him sitting at the city gate, where he has garnered enough esteem to become part of Sodom's leadership. Like his uncle Abraham, Lot offers hospitality to two approaching visitors. Lot lives in a community where sleeping in the public square places a person's morals—and perhaps his life—at risk, so Lot strongly insists that the visitors sleep at his house and kindly prepares a meal for them. After this meal, all the males of Sodom surround Lot's house and make a terrible demand: *"Where are the men who came to you tonight? Bring them out to us, that we may know them."* Jude 1:7 says, *"Sodom and Gomorrah and the surrounding cities, which likewise indulged in sexual immorality and pursued unnatural desire, serve as an example by undergoing a punishment of eternal fire."*

Lot attempts to protect his visitors by offering the crowd his two virgin daughters, even though the multitude clearly wants men. His proposal is met with contempt. The Sodomites are prepared to break down the door, but God's messengers are there to protect Lot. Abraham's prayers are effective on behalf of Sodom's only righteous inhabitant. The angels impose a divine judgment on the Sodomites, striking them with blindness.

Deliverance: Rescue Provided

The angels inform Lot that they are about to destroy the city because of its rampant wickedness. They urge him to evacuate his family and others for whom he bears responsibility. Lot attempts to warn his sons-in-law, urging them to *"Get out of this place, for the Lord is about to destroy the city."* Nothing could be plainer. His sons-in-law, however, do not take him seriously. In the end only Lot's wife and daughters leave with him, and only because the angels physically force them out of the city.

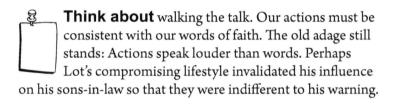

Think about walking the talk. Our actions must be consistent with our words of faith. The old adage still stands: Actions speak louder than words. Perhaps Lot's compromising lifestyle invalidated his influence on his sons-in-law so that they were indifferent to his warning.

With grave urgency, the angels direct Lot's family toward the mountains to the east. However, Lot is reluctant to leave the valley. He says—in spite of angelic help at his side—that he cannot reach the hill country before the disaster overtakes him. He asks that the tiny town of Zoar (meaning *insignificant*) be spared the coming destruction. The angels, acting under divine direction, grant Lot his request and agree to spare Zoar and to allow him to escape there. They insist that he move rapidly; God's judgment is being held back solely to accommodate his travel plans. Sodom has been a barrier to Lot's spiritual growth, yet he cannot drag himself away from it entirely.

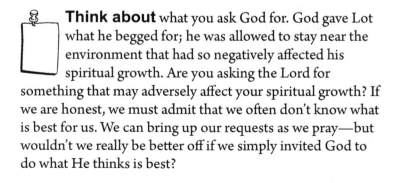

Think about what you ask God for. God gave Lot what he begged for; he was allowed to stay near the environment that had so negatively affected his spiritual growth. Are you asking the Lord for something that may adversely affect your spiritual growth? If we are honest, we must admit that we often don't know what is best for us. We can bring up our requests as we pray—but wouldn't we really be better off if we simply invited God to do what He thinks is best?

As soon as Lot reaches Zoar, God unleashes supernatural destruction upon Sodom and Gomorrah and the other cities—except Zoar. Even the lush vegetation that had first attracted Lot to the region is destroyed along with the residents. Lot's wife's attraction to Sodom—or perhaps a strange curiosity about the details of the judgment—proves too much for her. She looks back despite instructions not to do so and perishes as a result. The description that *"she became a pillar of salt"* does not necessarily mean she was transformed instantly into salt. God could have changed her in a moment's time, or, by lingering, she may have placed herself beneath the falling sulfur that overtook the area. After her death, her body would have been slowly encapsulated by the blowing salt that covers objects in the region even today.

Abraham rises early the next day to see what has happened. Returning to his valley overlook, he sees the dense smoke that marks the destruction of Sodom and Gomorrah. Confident of *Yahweh's* justice, Abraham no doubt mourns the destruction, but he knows that God would have *"remembered"* his petitions and removed Lot from the danger.

Decadence: Lot and His Daughters

Zoar fails to be the haven Lot and his daughters had hoped for; *"he was afraid to live"* there. They soon move east, to the mountains near the Dead Sea, and live in a cave. There they face an uncertain future, isolated from the life they have known and outside any settled social structures.

Because both daughters' betrothed husbands died in Sodom, the older daughter proposes to her sister a solution to what appears to be the imminent end of their family line: have Lot impregnate her. Knowing he would never agree to such wickedness while sober, they get him drunk. The next night, the younger daughter is impregnated as well. The child conceived by the elder daughter is named Moab; that of the younger daughter, *Ben-Ammi*. Their descendants, the Moabites and Ammonites, will persistently trouble the Israelites for many generations. Lot and his descendants pay a steep price for settling in Sodom.

Personalize this lesson.

☑ Lot almost certainly never wanted or anticipated having daughters whose relationship with God would be so distant that they would trick him into participating in incestuous relations with them. He surely never intended for his wife to become so enamored with the world that she would die rather than flee from judgment. He never planned to live in a city inhabited exclusively by people who had utterly turned their backs to God. But smaller, seemingly innocent choices, such as making his own desires paramount in dividing the land with his uncle, moved him down a gradual path that led to disaster. The farther he went down that path, the harder it was to turn back. Will you resolve to regularly examine your spiritual path and be willing to turn around if you see it leading you in the wrong direction? Consider investing a day in prayer to examine your life so that He can re-direct your steps as needed.

God Fulfills His Promise
Genesis 20–21

❖ Genesis 20:1-7—God Preserves the Sanctity of Abraham's Marriage

1. How are the circumstances of this passage similar to the situation described in Genesis 12:11-20?

    _____

    _____

    _____

2. What does the fact that a 90-year-old woman was desired in a harem suggest God may have done to prepare Sarah to bear a child?

    _____

    _____

3. How does God rescue Sarah from a situation that could have compromised the legitimacy of the son God had promised?

    _____

    _____

4. What does Genesis 12:1-3 record God doing to confirm that Abraham is still the man He has chosen to bless and to use to bless others?

    _____

    _____

    _____

❖ Genesis 20:8-18—God Vindicates the God-Fearer

5. How does Abimelech respond to God's command?

    _____

    _____

6. What does this tell us about his heart? (Also see Proverbs 21:1.)

    _____

    _____

    _____

7. What excuses does Abraham make when Abimelech asks why he lied?

    _____

    _____

    _____

8. Has your faith ever wavered when circumstances seemed uncertain or threatening? If so, will you share the outcome of this experience with study group members or a friend?

    _____

    _____

    _____

9. What attributes of God are displayed in this passage?

    _____

    _____

    _____

10. Choose one of these attributes and tell how God has demonstrated this attribute in your life.

    _____

    _____

    _____

❖ Genesis 21:1-7—God Fulfills the Promise of a Son

11. How old are Abraham and Sarah when the son God promised is born? (Also see Genesis 17:17.)

    _____

12. How long had they waited for this child after he was first promised? (See Genesis 12:1-4.)

    _____

13. How would you describe Sarah's feelings after the miraculous birth of her child?

    _____

    _____

    _____

14. The name *Isaac* means *laughter*. Why is this name especially appropriate for this child? (See Genesis 17:17-19; 18:10-15; 21:6.)

    _____

    _____

    _____

❖ Genesis 21:8-21—God Removes the Threat to Isaac's Inheritance

15. How does Ishmael's attitude toward Isaac confirm God's prophecy in Genesis 16:12?

    _____

    _____

16. Sarah demands that Abraham send Ishmael away. What potential threat to her son does she see?

    _____

    _____

    _____

17. Why does God overrule Abraham and support Sarah in this matter?

_____

_____

❖ Genesis 21:22-34—Abraham Offers His Neighbor Peace

18. Why does Abimelech want to enter into a treaty with Abraham?

_____

_____

19. How has your relationship with God affected your relationships with family, friends and business associates?

_____

_____

_____

_____

Apply what you have learned. Does it seem to you that Abraham took too long to learn some important lessons about simply trusting God and not resorting to deception? God had great patience with Abraham. Be encouraged that He is patient with us also. Ask God to bring to your memory a time when He intervened for you when you messed up. Then thank Him for His kindness and patience. Let that remembrance stir up a deeper love for and trust in our faithful God.

God Fulfills His Promise
Genesis 20–21

After a quarter-century of waiting, Abraham and Sarah are blessed by Isaac's arrival. However, first an embarrassing episode occurs involving King Abimelech. After the promised heir is born, Ishmael's presence causes conflict and leads to Hagar and Ishmael's exile.

God Preserves the Sanctity of Abraham's Marriage

Soon after God's announcement of Isaac's birth, but before Sarah becomes pregnant, Abraham is living in a region of the Negev controlled by the Philistine king Abimelech, who covets Sarah for his harem. He feels free to take her because Abraham has resorted to his half-truth of claiming that Sarah is his sister, as he did 25 years earlier in Egypt.

God moves immediately to maintain the couple's marriage by appearing to the Philistine king in a dream, reproving him in language that strikes terror in his heart: *"Behold, you are a dead man because of the woman whom you have taken, for she is a man's wife"* (20:3). Abimelech pleads that Abraham and Sarah lied to him. God acknowledges this claim, adding that Abimelech's failure to violate Sarah was due to God supernaturally restraining him. Abimelech must return Sarah to Abraham. Despite Abraham's sin, God identifies him as a prophet—the first use of the term in the Bible—saying that Abraham *"will pray for you and you shall live."*

God Vindicates the Integrity of the God-Fearer

Again, a pagan rebukes Abraham for his dishonesty. Abimelech calls Abraham to account for his lie: *"How have I sinned against you, that you have brought on me and my kingdom a great sin? You have done to me things that ought not to be done"* (20:9).

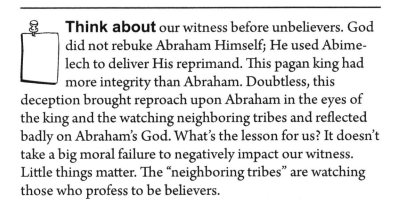

Think about our witness before unbelievers. God did not rebuke Abraham Himself; He used Abimelech to deliver His reprimand. This pagan king had more integrity than Abraham. Doubtless, this deception brought reproach upon Abraham in the eyes of the king and the watching neighboring tribes and reflected badly on Abraham's God. What's the lesson for us? It doesn't take a big moral failure to negatively impact our witness. Little things matter. The "neighboring tribes" are watching those who profess to be believers.

Abraham offers three excuses. First, he feared for his life. Second, Sarah actually is his half sister. Third, he had requested that Sarah lie to demonstrate her love. Certainly none of Abraham's reasons would impress God, but Abimelech refuses to contest them and determines to compensate Abraham. As in the case of Pharaoh, 25 years earlier, Abimelech's gifts are lavish: livestock and slaves and the invitation to live anywhere he likes within the king's domain. The king vindicates Sarah's honor by giving Abraham 1,000 pieces of silver as *"a sign of your innocence."*

As God promised, Abraham prays for Abimelech. The females of Abimelech's household become barren the moment Sarah enters the harem. Abraham's prayer releases God's healing, and Abimelech's household returns to normal.

Also, Abraham's marriage is restored at this crucial point. Although Abraham was unfaithful, God remained faithful (2 Timothy 2:13).

God Fulfills His Promise of a Son

At last, after 25 years of waiting, *"the Lord did to Sarah as He had promised."* The longed-for son finally arrives, and at the very time God had predicted. In keeping with God's word, the boy is named *Isaac,* which means *he laughs.* At the proper age of eight days, he is circumcised and made a child of the covenant.

Some people take God at His word in simple faith. Others, like Sarah, find that learning to trust God is a never-ending process. When she first hears she is to become a mother, Sarah snickers skeptically. Now that

Isaac has actually arrived, her laughter is transformed to genuine joy. Sarah's experience displays God's grace: *"The Lord visited Sarah as He had said."* She initially stumbled at God's promise despite His many past favors, but eventually recognized her own unbelief and overcame it: *"By faith Sarah herself received power to conceive, even when she was past the age, since she considered Him faithful who had promised"* (Hebrews 11:11).

God Removes the Threat to Isaac's Inheritance

Genesis 21:8 moves Isaac's story ahead several years. During a feast Sarah notices Ishmael, who is about 16 years old, *"laughing"* at Isaac. After the guests leave, she demands, *"Cast out this slave woman with her son, for the son of this slave woman shall not be heir with my son Isaac."* Abraham is relieved when God assumes full responsibility for Ishmael's welfare: *"I will make a nation of the son of the slave woman also, because he is your offspring."*

Abraham provides Hagar and Ishmael with food and water and sends them away. They roam the inhospitable region of the Negev around Beersheba. Finally, exhausted and without supplies, they stop to weep, and to die. That's when God speaks, assuring Hagar that Ishmael has a distinguished future: *"I will make him into a great nation."* Then God reveals a nearby well; its water will revive them. Ishmael would become a man of distinction, living along the western edge of the Promised Land and eventually marrying an Egyptian woman.

Abraham Offers His Neighbors Peace

Because God is blessing Abraham, Abimelech seeks a peace treaty with him. He asks for an oath before Abraham's God that the prophet will deal truly with him. While they are talking, Abraham mentions that Abimelech's servants have seized a well that Abraham had dug long ago. Abimelech claims no knowledge of this and soon restores the well. The two leaders draw up a second agreement over the well. The location is named *Beersheba,* meaning, *well of the oath.*

Personalize this lesson.

☑ As believers, *"our citizenship is in heaven"* (Philippians 3:20). We are to sojourn in this world while possessing a strong attachment to another homeland. Abraham was promised the entire land of Canaan, but died owning very little of it. *"By faith he went to live in the land of promise, as in a foreign land, living in tents with Isaac and Jacob, heirs with him of the same promise. For he was looking forward to the city that has foundations, whose designer and builder is God"* (Hebrews 11:9-10). Consider your future, sojourner: One day you will reside in heaven, no longer a resident alien on this earth, but home forever with God. And won't it be great to share experiences with Abraham? Meanwhile, what are some actions you can take to make this alien land more like heaven for those you influence?

God Tests Abraham
Genesis 22:1-19

Memorize God's Word: Genesis 22:8a.

❖ Genesis 22:1-8—Abraham Faces His Greatest Test

1. In Genesis 22:1-2, what did God command Abraham to do?

    _____

    _____

2. What was His purpose?

    _____

    _____

    _____

3. Without knowing God's purpose at this time, what options did Abraham face when God gave him this command?

    _____

    _____

    _____

4. If God already knew how Abraham would respond, why would He ask Abraham to do such a thing? (See Isaiah 48:10.)

    _____

    _____

    _____

5. Besides the personal suffering and consequences involved in obeying God's command, what spiritual dilemma was Abraham also dealing with? (See Genesis 17:4-7, 19.)

_____

_____

_____

6. What details in this passage reveal Abraham's resolute faith in God even though he couldn't possibly have understood God's reasons for asking him to do this?

_____

_____

_____

7. Was Abraham being deceptive when he gave the instructions to his servants recorded in verse 5? What was he relying on? (See also Hebrews 11:17-19.)

_____

_____

_____

8. How does his answer to Isaac's question in verses 7-8 also reveal his unwavering faith in God?

_____

_____

9. How does the Bible define *faith* in Hebrews 11:1, 6?

_____

_____

10. How does Abraham's obedience in this passage exemplify this concept?

_____

_____

_____

❖ Genesis 22:9-14—Abraham Offers God His Greatest Gift

11. What final steps of obedience does Abraham take in verses 9-10?

_____

_____

12. What does this passage lead us to assume about Isaac's attitude toward his father and toward God?

_____

_____

_____

13. When and how does God intervene in this heart-wrenching test?

_____

_____

14. What evidence do we find in Abraham's actions that prove he has genuine faith? (See also James 2:21-24.)

_____

_____

_____

❖ Genesis 22:15-19—God Reconfirms His Promise of Blessing

15. Why do you think God reconfirms His promises to Abraham at this time?

_____

_____

_____

16. By whose name does God take this oath, and why? (See Hebrews 6:13-17.)

_____

_____

17. What promises to those who believe in His Son does God confirm in the following passages?

     a.   John 14:1-3 _____

        _____

     b.   Romans 8:38-39 _____

        _____

     c.   Ephesians 1:13-14 _____

        _____

❖ Selected Passages—God Sacrifices His Own Son

18. Reread Genesis 22:1-19.

     a.   How are Abraham's actions in this chapter a picture of God's sacrificial love for us? (See John 3:16; Romans 8:32.)

        _____

        _____

     b.   How does Isaac's attitude in this episode illustrate Christ's love for and submission to His Father? (See Matthew 26:42; John 18:11.)

        _____

        _____

Apply what you have learned. Imagine Isaac's thoughts when he climbed onto the altar and allowed his father to tie him up. He could have refused. Even when Abraham *"took the knife to slaughter his son"* (22:10), the Scriptures don't indicate that he offered any resistance. What a perfect picture of Jesus' attitude when He prayed in Gethsemane, *"not My will, but Yours, be done"* (Luke 22:42). When the Father calls you, as His child, *"to present your bod[y] as a living sacrifice, holy and acceptable to God"* (Romans 12:1) will you refuse or resist? What sacrifice is God calling you to make?

God Tests Abraham
Genesis 22:1-19

While still in the region of Beersheba, Abraham faces his most difficult test. God asks him to sacrifice the son for whom he had waited so many years. In meeting this challenge, Abraham shows great spiritual maturity, and God gives him a new set of promises.

Abraham Prepares to Sacrifice Isaac

Isaac is probably in his mid-to-late teens when this scene occurs. Genesis 22:1 reveals Abraham is being tested. Will he demonstrate the reality of his faith in God by the radical obedience God calls for?

Think about why God tests us. God does not test us to make us fail but rather to see us succeed. Because faith is like a muscle and must be used to grow strong, God tests us to give us the opportunity to exercise our faith. Moreover, He tests us so we can know the strength of our faith. If you are going through a test right now, consider what God might want to do in your life by allowing it. And consider the heart attitude God desires for us to have during the test: *"Count it all joy, my brothers, when you meet trials of various kinds, for you know that the testing of your faith produces steadfastness. And let steadfastness have its full effect, that you may be perfect and complete, lacking in nothing"* (James 1:2-4). It may be hard to rejoice while being tested, but pondering the potential results should help.

The emphasis in 22:2 lies on the closeness between Abraham and Isaac: *"your son, your only son, Isaac, whom you love."* The word *son* appears

11 times in Genesis 22:2-16. God is asking Abraham to demonstrate whether his love for his son exceeds his love for God. For this supreme test of his life, the patriarch is told to go to the area known as Moriah. It is a northward extension of the ridge upon which the city of David was built. The place where Abraham offers Isaac would later serve as the location of Israel's sacrifices. It is also close to the place where God would one day sacrifice His Son.

Abraham arises *"early in the morning."* Knowing that the region of Moriah has little in the way of usable firewood, he cuts wood in advance and brings it on the trip, which requires a three-day walk.

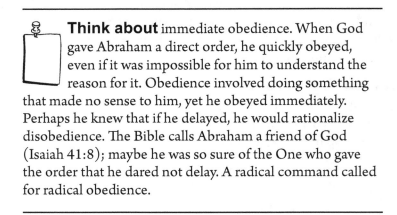

Think about immediate obedience. When God gave Abraham a direct order, he quickly obeyed, even if it was impossible for him to understand the reason for it. Obedience involved doing something that made no sense to him, yet he obeyed immediately. Perhaps he knew that if he delayed, he would rationalize disobedience. The Bible calls Abraham a friend of God (Isaiah 41:8); maybe he was so sure of the One who gave the order that he dared not delay. A radical command called for radical obedience.

When he finally sees the location, Abraham leaves his servants behind, telling them, *"Stay here with the donkey; I and the boy will go over there and worship and come again to you."* He knows that Isaac will return with him. The writer of Hebrews states, *"By faith Abraham, when he was tested, offered up Isaac, and he who had received the promises was in the act of offering up his only son, of whom it was said, 'Through Isaac shall your offspring be named.' He considered that God was able even to raise him from the dead, from which, figuratively speaking, he did receive him back"* (Hebrews 11:17-19).

It cannot be emphasized too strongly that Abraham endures this test because of his faith in God's revealed truth. God speaks to him in words that are unmistakable, even providing specific travel directions. Once God's orders are clear, Abraham acts promptly. He does so although the thought of bringing harm to his beloved son must be dreadful. When Isaac notes that the main ingredient of a whole burnt offering—the sacrificial animal—is missing, Abraham's response is both accurate and evasive: God will supply His own sacrifice.

God Substitutes a Ram for Isaac

Little is made of Isaac's emotions during the ordeal; he seems to trust his father completely. At the moment of execution, the Angel of the LORD, always presumed to be the pre-incarnate Christ, urgently calls *"Abraham, Abraham!"*

Abraham fears and reverences God as Sovereign Lord from whom he will withhold nothing. The most horrible thought imaginable to Abraham is the possibility of offending the God he loves and serves. If God asks for sacrifice, he would give it without regard to his personal pain or loss. No higher calling exists in Scripture than the command to love the Lord with *"all your heart and with all your soul and with all your might"* (Deuteronomy 6:5).

True to his own predictions, Abraham gladly observes a ram caught in a thicket nearby. This animal is offered *"instead of"* Isaac. What God does not require of Abraham, He would one day demand of Himself. Near the same spot, His own Son would die as a humanity's substitute. Abraham commemorates the occasion by naming the place *Yahweh-Jireh,* meaning *"the* LORD *will provide."*

In recognition of this great turning point, the Angel of the LORD calls to Abraham again from heaven. Because of Abraham's devotion, God has decided to swear an oath, confirming His previous promises of blessing. As before, God emphasizes to Abraham that he and his offspring have been chosen not only to receive divine blessings, but to dispense them to *"all nations of the earth."*

God Demonstrates His Love for Us Through Abraham and Isaac

This is the only place in the Old Testament that distinctly teaches—in typology—that God will require the sacrifice of a beloved Son—a human sacrifice—for divine justice to be satisfied. God the Father, recognizing the terrible pain Abraham would feel, reveals His own heartbreak over having to sacrifice His only Son in order to offer us forgiveness (Matthew 3:17). No animal sacrifice would suffice. Humanity sinned, and a human, the God-Man, must pay the wages of sin (Romans 6:23).

Personalize this lesson.

☑ In the Hebrew, Abraham speaks only one word in response to God's call to him to sacrifice his son (Genesis 22:1, 11): *Hineni*! Translated, the word means *Here I am* or *I am ready*, but it is rich with meaning in the Hebrew. When God called Moses (Exodus 3:4) and Isaiah (Isaiah 6:8), both replied *Hineni*! The word implies a father-child relationship. The child is fully open to the Father's commands, fully trusting that whatever the Father calls His child to do will bring glory to Him and spiritual satisfaction to the child. What lifestyle changes are you willing to make so that when God calls, you will be ready to say "Yes" to Him?

Abraham the Sojourner
Genesis 22:20-23:20

❖ Genesis 22:20-24—The Family Abraham Left Behind

1. The passage gives a brief description of another "branch" of Abraham's family tree. What did Genesis 11:27-32 reveal about this branch of the family?

   _____

   _____

   _____

2. What new information does Genesis 22:20-24 give us about this family?

   _____

   _____

3. Why is it significant to the Bible's account of Abraham? (See also Genesis 24:15, 67.)

   _____

   _____

4. Because children, and especially sons, were symbols of success in the ancient Near East, how do you think Abraham might have felt when he compared his brother's life with his own?

   _____

   _____

   _____

5. What are some of the symbols of success in our culture?

    _____

    _____

❖ Genesis 23:1-2—The Death and Legacy of Sarah

6. What godly qualities does Peter attribute to Sarah in his
    discussion of godly wives in 1 Peter 3:1-6?

    _____

    _____

7. What qualities do you find in Sarah—godly or otherwise—in
    these scenes from her life?

    a. Genesis 12:1-5 _____

    _____

    _____

    b. Genesis 12:10-20 _____

    _____

    _____

    c. Genesis 16:1-6 _____

    _____

    _____

    d. Genesis 17:3-8, 15-16 (Look for a blessing, not a quality, in
        this one.) _____

    _____

    _____

    e. Genesis 18:10-15 _____

    _____

    _____

    f. Genesis 21:1-13 _____

    _____

    _____

8. What lessons can we learn from this remarkable woman's life?

_____

_____

❖ Genesis 23:3-18—Burial of Sarah

9. What request does Abraham make of the local residents when Sarah dies?

_____

_____

10. What final terms do Abraham and Ephron agree upon?

_____

_____

11. How do they complete the transaction?

_____

_____

12. What do you learn about Abraham from this transaction?

_____

_____

❖ Genesis 23:19-20—Commitment to the Promised Land

In Abraham's culture, people were buried in their homeland.

13. Who is later buried in Machpelah Cave? (See Genesis 49:29-31.)

_____

_____

14. Who is determined to be buried in the Promised Land? (See Genesis 50:24-25 and Exodus 13:19.)

_____

_____

15. How does Abraham's purchase of Ephron's field and cave demonstrate his faith in God's promise seen in Genesis 15?

_____

_____

16. In what practical, visible ways can you demonstrate your faith in God's promises to you?

_____

_____

Apply what you have learned. Instead of going back home to Ur, Abraham purchases a cave in Canaan in which to bury his beloved Sarah. Abraham is ensuring that his family truly "occupies" the Promised Land, just as God commanded him to do. He and his progeny will be buried at Machpelah as well. By this, Abraham is declaring that he knows God's promises extend beyond this life and that his people will inherit God's eternal promises. Like Abraham, we hope in resurrection because our hope is Jesus Christ who is *"the resurrection and the life. Whoever believes in Me, though he die, yet shall he live, and everyone who lives and believes in Me shall never die"* (John 11:25-26). How is your hope in the resurrection changing your life?

Abraham the Sojourner
Genesis 22:20-23:20

When Abraham is 137 and Isaac 37, Sarah dies. Her death forces a decision on the grieving patriarch. Where will he bury his wife? Through a difficult negotiation with a Hittite inhabitant of Canaan, Abraham buys a portion of the land God has promised him and buries his beloved Sarah.

The Family Abraham Left Behind

Abraham learns that, in contrast to the few children born to him, his elder brother, Nahor, has produced not only eight sons through his wife, but four more through Reumah, his concubine. The last of these, Bethuel, is the father of Rebekah, the woman who will become Isaac's bride.

Abraham is finally faced with the loss of his beloved Sarah, who dies in Hebron at the age of 127. He weeps over his loss of Sarah. This marks the Bible's first recording of a man's tears—but not the last.

Think about how a Christian grieves. In the New Testament, Paul calls death *"the last enemy"* (1 Corinthians 15:26). The terrible sense of loss, separation, and loneliness when a loved one dies are natural human feelings. However, believers know that loved ones who die in the faith are in a far better place. They are with Jesus—*"away from the body and at home with the Lord"* (2 Corinthians 5:8). One day we will join them there, hallelujah!

As Abraham grieves, he faces a difficult decision. The custom in those days was to bury honored dead near their relatives in their homeland.

Is his home in Haran or in the Promised Land of Canaan? He decides he will not return Sarah to Paddan Aram, but bury her in the Promised Land, testifying to her children and grandchildren of her trust in God. That decision poses a difficulty, however. Abraham owns none of the land that God has promised him.

Abraham goes to *"the Hittites"* and pleads: *"give me property ... for a burying place"* (Genesis 23:4). The Hittites recognize Abraham's prominence in the area, addressing him as *"a prince of God"* living among them, but are reluctant to sell him anything. Instead, they propose to allow Sarah to be buried in one of their own tombs, adding that the entire community would be pleased to share their property with him. The Patriarch shows deference to these leaders, but he finds their proposal unacceptable. It is time to put down roots in the Promised Land. He wants some acreage of his own. Throughout the negotiations, Abraham seems careful to make sure that his attitude and his words commend rather than detract from his testimony before these pagans.

Think about politeness as a virtue. Neglecting niceties appears to be a cultural trend; people feel free to say or do exactly what they are thinking, no matter how rude. This is not God's way. Paul makes God's principle very clear: *"Don't give offense to Jews or Gentiles or the church of God. I, too, try to please everyone in everything I do. I don't just do what is best for me; I do what is best for others so that many may be saved"* (1 Corinthians 10:32-33, NLT). A little "uncommon" courtesy just might open the door for sharing our faith.

Abraham offers a counterproposal: Perhaps they could help him negotiate the purchase of a particular cave belonging to a prominent Hittite leader, Ephron. Abraham offers to buy the cave, located at the end of a large field owned by Ephron, for the full purchase value. Soon Abraham is involved in direct negotiations with Ephron at *"the gate of his city,"* the location where the law courts sit and city business is conducted. As was the custom in the ancient East, Ephron displays extraordinary generosity, offering to give not only the cave, but the field attached to it to Abraham for nothing. Had Abraham been so bold as to accept this offer, it is likely that Ephron would have backtracked rapidly. The ritual has to be carried out to its logical conclusion for the sake of form, however. Abraham knows this and plays the game to its end. He is acutely conscious that not only Ephron but the entire community is evaluating his negotiations, so he again *"bowed down before the people of the land"* (23:12) who are sitting as silent observers. Finally, he asks for a specific amount: What is the full value of the field?

Even as Ephron quotes the exorbitant price of 400 shekels of silver, Ephron pretends that Abraham's payment of any price at all is purely the patriarch's option. Abraham agrees and gives Ephron the silver. In time, he receives the registered title to the property, with the merchants and officials looking on at the city gate. Sarah is laid to rest in the cave, where, eventually, Abraham, Leah, Isaac, Rebekah, and Jacob would join her.

A commentary on Abraham's pilgrim mentality is found in Hebrews 11:13-16: *"These all died in faith, not having received the things promised, but having seen them and greeted them from afar, and having acknowledged that they were strangers and exiles on the earth. For people who speak thus make it clear that they are seeking a homeland. If they had been thinking of that land from which they had gone out, they would have had opportunity to return. But as it is, they desire a better country, that is, a heavenly one. Therefore God is not ashamed to be called their God, for He has prepared for them a city."*

While believers are to live as *"strangers and exiles on the earth,"* separation from the values and priorities of the present age does not mean indifference to the fate of the people and culture of this age. Virtually without exception, the heroes of faith mentioned in Hebrews 11 enriched the lives of those around them and left the world they lived in a better place. They did so not because they thought better economic or cultural conditions formed ends in themselves. They desired to bring glory to God, and in the process display His love and faithfulness.

Personalize this lesson.

☑ What made the Hittites call Abraham *"a prince of God"* at the ripe old age of 137? His physique? Doubtful! Isn't it more likely his regal spirit? Abraham and Sarah's attractiveness as they grew older is something that we can have if we walk with God as they did. The fruit of the Spirit—*"love, joy, peace, patience, kindness, goodness, faithfulness, gentleness, self-control"* (Galatians 5:22-23)—spilling over in our lives is guaranteed to make us look good to God, and perhaps even to our friends and family! You cannot earn the fruit of the Spirit, but you can do things to cultivate and display it. What habits could you cultivate, starting this week, that will in turn cultivate and display the fruit of the Spirit in your life, to the benefit of others?

Marks of a Successful Servant
Genesis 24

Memorize God's Word: Genesis 24:12.

❖ Genesis 24:1-9—Committed Devotion

1. a. What responsibility does Abraham entrust to his servant?

   _____

   _____

   b. What qualifications does the servant have for this job?

   _____

   _____

2. What makes this task especially important? (Review Genesis 9:24-25; 22:17-18.)

   _____

   _____

   _____

3. Why doesn't Abraham do the task himself?

   _____

   _____

4. How does Abraham emphasize the critical nature of this mission?

   _____

   _____

   _____

5. What two major concerns does Abraham outline in his instructions to the servant?

    _____

    _____

6. How does Abraham answer the servant's concern about what to do if the woman is unwilling to come back?

    _____

    _____

❖ Genesis 24:10-27—Prayerful Obedience

7. a. What strategy does the servant employ as he begins his search for a wife for Isaac?

    _____

    _____

    b. Whose help does he enlist and what signs does he ask for?

    _____

    _____

8. How could these signs be not only definitive, but also practical in identifying the wife God has chosen for Isaac?

    _____

    _____

9. How does the servant know he has found the right girl?

    _____

10. a. What qualities does the servant demonstrate in this passage?

    _____

    _____

    b. Which of these qualities are also necessary for us if we want to serve God successfully? Explain.

    _____

    _____

❖ Genesis 24:28-49—Sincere Faithfulness

11. Who seems to be in charge in Rebekah's household? What is your impression of him?

_____

_____

12. How does the servant demonstrate his single-minded faithfulness to Abraham in this passage?

_____

_____

13. Why do you think the servant shared the particular details he did about Abraham's circumstances and family?

_____

_____

14. How does his account of his search reveal his personal awe and reverence for God?

_____

_____

❖ Genesis 24:50-67—Extraordinary Success

15. How does Rebekah's family respond to the servant's request?

_____

_____

16. What factors do you think influenced their decision?

_____

_____

17. How does their farewell blessing on Rebekah correspond to God's plan for Abraham and his offspring? (See also Genesis 12:2; 15:4-5.)

_____

_____

18. How would you describe Isaac and Rebekah's initial meeting?

_____

_____

❖ Genesis 24:1-67—An Example to Follow

19. What principles for discovering God's will can we learn from this chapter?

_____

_____

20. What principles for successful service in the kingdom of God can we learn?

_____

_____

Apply what you have learned. Have you ever wanted to know some simple, plain steps for finding God's will? Here they are in chapter 24 of Genesis! First, you must really want God's will, not just say you do. Abraham earnestly wanted a godly wife for Isaac—the next link in the promised chain from Abraham to Messiah. He knew that a godly wife would be found among his family, not among the pagan Canaanites, so he sent his servant back to his country. The servant obeyed his master, just as God expects us to obey when He speaks to us through His Word. And the servant prayed specific prayers for guidance. Then he watched for God to act. The instant Rebekah showed up, *"the servant ran to meet her."* Will you ask God to help you take steps to develop a spiritual sense of hearing that clearly discerns and eagerly responds to His directions?

Lesson 16 Commentary

Marks of a Successful Servant
Genesis 24

Genesis 24 describes how Abraham finds a suitable bride for Isaac. The patriarch commissions his most trusted servant to return to his birth country to seek God's choice for Isaac's wife. The servant portrays the role of the Holy Spirit, who does not speak of Himself, but only of the Son, whose interests He represents.

Committed Devotion

Abraham is 140 years old when the chapter opens. Though Isaac is now about 40 years old, it is still his father's role to arrange a suitable marriage. Abraham, being too old to travel, assigns his faithful servant to represent him to his relatives in Aram Naharaim. This unnamed *"servant"* proves to be the central figure and hero as the drama unfolds.

Under no circumstances must Isaac marry a Canaanite woman, all of whom lack faith in the true God. God, who had been so faithful in the past, would not abandon Abraham now: *"He will send His angel before you, and you shall take a wife for my son from there"* (24:7). In the unlikely event that the servant finds no willing candidate, he should consider himself released from his oath. Twice, however, Abraham warns his servant, *"You must not take my son back there"* (24:6, 8).

Prayerful Obedience

Abraham's servant begins his journey by preparing 10 camels for the trip, several of which bear presents for the bride-to-be and her family. These gifts will show the groom's financial well-being. The servant's destination is the town where Nahor, Abraham's brother, lives. After a trip of some 500 miles, Abraham's servant halts the caravan at the local public well. Then he appeals to *Yahweh* to identify the girl by having her offer water not just to him but also to his camels. Drawing water for 10 camels involved a considerable amount of work, and for a young woman to take the initiative to do so for a stranger would be unlikely.

Even before the servant's brief prayer is over, a beautiful young woman named Rebekah comes to the well. The servant must have held his breath as Rebekah, almost as though she were reading lines from a script, played out her part in answer to his prayer. After waiting until all the camels are watered, the servant prepares to give Rebekah expensive gifts from his master's treasure. First, however, he makes the critical request: *"Please tell me whose daughter you are"* (24:23). Rebekah confirms his hopes when she replies that she is the granddaughter of Nahor and that her family would be glad to host the servant and his companions for the night. The servant immediately proclaims his gratitude to Yahweh, who has so quickly and clearly answered his prayers.

Sincere Faithfulness

Rebekah quickly informs the household of the visitor and his mission. Her brother Laban addresses Abraham's servant as, *"blessed of the LORD"* (24:31). This phrase suggests that he and the servant both worship *Yahweh*. Laban, however, is always ready to seek any advantage, especially in financial matters. In a later chapter, he will exhibit unusual devotion to a set of household idols. For the moment, he shows kindness by providing a meal for his guests. But Abraham's devoted servant refuses even to eat until he reveals the purpose of his mission.

The servant is careful to point out that Isaac, the son who was born to his master late in life, is now Abraham's sole heir. If the servant finds a young woman who is faithful to *Yahweh*, he is ready on behalf of his master to be generous with her family if they will consent to her marriage to Isaac. The servant serves his master sincerely, omitting nothing that is in Abraham's interest. He ends his explanation by describing his prayer for divine guidance and the remarkable way it was answered in the person of Rebekah. He only wants to know if they will *"show steadfast love and faithfulness"* (24:49) to his master. His concern is to follow the Lord's leading, and if they do not share that concern, he will be on his way.

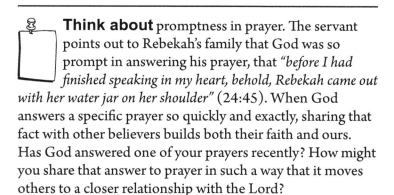

Think about promptness in prayer. The servant points out to Rebekah's family that God was so prompt in answering his prayer, that *"before I had finished speaking in my heart, behold, Rebekah came out with her water jar on her shoulder"* (24:45). When God answers a specific prayer so quickly and exactly, sharing that fact with other believers builds both their faith and ours. Has God answered one of your prayers recently? How might you share that answer to prayer in such a way that it moves others to a closer relationship with the Lord?

Extraordinary Success

Laban and Bethuel concur that God has expressed His will; they agree to the marriage. The servant then bows in submission and thanksgiving to *Yahweh*. Then he provides costly gifts for Rebekah and for her brother and mother. Having found success on his mission, the servant and his group enjoy a meal with Bethuel's family and stay overnight.

The family wisely decides to consult Rebekah concerning the matter. She, like the servant, shows her confidence in Yahweh by agreeing to go immediately on the long journey to Canaan. The family encourages her by sending along her personal servants. They also pronounce a blessing on her. It is their hope that her children will be numbered in the *"thousands of ten thousands"* (24:60), a blessing that has been fulfilled many times over.

As the caravan arrives in Canaan, Isaac is visible in the distance. Rebekah dismounts from her camel and covers herself with a veil. The servant affirms God's involvement in his entire experience, and Isaac brings her into Sarah's tent. The act is important, for it is the only wedding ceremony typically observed by nomadic peoples at this time. The author notes that in his doing so *"she became his wife"* (24:67). God's choice is always perfect: Isaac *"loved her ... [and] was comforted after his mother's death."*

Personalize this lesson.

How does God guide? Among the many ways He leads are through the canon of Scripture, through the wise counsel of mature believers, through the circumstances and "divine coincidences" in our lives, through our consciences, and through His Holy Spirit. If you honestly don't know what to do, ask again and wait. You might pray, "Lord show me Your will, and if You already showed me and I missed it, please show me again." Then, like Rebekah, just do it!

The Death and Descendants of Abraham
Genesis 25

❖ Genesis 25:1-18—The Sons of Abraham

NOTE: Moses, the writer of Genesis, does not tell us when Abraham took another wife, only that he did. According to 1 Chronicles 1:32, Keturah was a concubine who functioned in much the same role as Hagar—that of providing sons to carry on the patriarch's name and work.

1. How many sons of Abraham are listed in this passage? Who are their mothers?

    _____

    _____

    _____

    _____

2. Which son is designated to retain possession of the birthright of God's covenant? (See also Genesis 17:19-21 and 21:12.) Who made that determination?

    _____

    _____

3. a. How does the Bible describe Abraham at his death? _____

    _____

    _____

    b. Where, and by whom, was he buried? _____

    _____

❖ Selected Passages—Lessons from Abraham's Life

4. What different facets of Abraham's character do the following passages reveal?

   a. Genesis 12:4; 17:23; 22:9-10 _____

   _____

   b. Genesis 12:8; 13:3-4, 18 _____

   _____

   c. Genesis 15:2-3, 8 _____

   _____

   d. Genesis 15:6; 22:8 _____

   _____

5. According to the following passages, what can we learn about Abraham as he faced the major decisions of his life?

   a. Genesis 12:10-13; 20:1-3, 11-13 _____

   _____

   b. Genesis 13:8-12 _____

   _____

   c. Genesis 14:21-23 _____

   _____

   d. Genesis 22:9-12 _____

   _____

6. According to the following verses, for what purposes in God's eternal plan was Abraham chosen?

   a. Genesis 12:1-3 _____

   _____

   b. Genesis 17:4-8 _____

   _____

   c. Genesis 18:19 _____

   _____

    d. Romans 4:11b-12 _____

        _____

7. What is the most important lesson you have learned from Abraham's life?

        _____

        _____

❖ Genesis 25:19-26—The Next Generation of the Covenant: Isaac's Twins

8. What does this passage tell us about the birth of Isaac's sons?

        _____

        _____

9. What prompted Rebekah to *"inquire of the LORD"* during her pregnancy (25:22)?

        _____

        _____

10. What plan did God reveal for her unborn sons at that time?

        _____

        _____

11. What does this plan tell us about God? (See also Romans 9:10-16.)

        _____

        _____

12. What do the following passages reveal about this quality of God?

    a. Isaiah 55:9 _____

        _____

    b. Daniel 4:37 _____

        _____

    c. Romans 9:10-21_____

        _____

❖ Genesis 25:27-34—The Birthright Abandoned and Seized

NOTE: In the Old Testament, the birthright included the firstborn son's right to a double portion of the inheritance as well as leadership of the family after the father's death.

13. How do the first two verses of this passage help set the stage for a lifetime of conflict between Isaac's sons?

_____

_____

14. What does Esau's attitude toward his birthright reveal about his character? (See also Hebrews 12:16-17.)

_____

_____

15. What can we learn about Jacob from this episode?

_____

_____

Apply what you have learned. Why did Jacob feel the need to "help God" and manipulate to assure himself of owning the family birthright? God had promised him the birthright before he was even born. All he had to do was wait. It was a "done deal." But he couldn't quite take God at His word. In what circumstances do you find it difficult to trust in and wait upon God? Stand on God's Word! *"Let us hold fast the confession of our hope without wavering, for He who promised is faithful"* (Hebrews 10:23).

The Death and Descendants of Abraham
Genesis 25

Genesis 25 introduces Jacob and Esau, who will dominate the next 11 chapters. Though twins, they could hardly have been more different. Even within their mother's womb, their struggles forecast the battles to come. Jacob will take advantage of his brother's tendency to choose immediate gratification at the expense of what is truly valuable.

The Descendants of Abraham Through Keturah

After Sarah's death, Abraham lives another 38 years and takes additional concubines. The only concubine identified by name, Keturah, bears Abraham six sons. Of these, Midian is noteworthy because his descendants will later take Joseph into Egypt and sell him as a slave. To emphasize that Isaac is his sole heir, Abraham gives Midian and his other sons monetary gifts and sends them away. The sons of Keturah and the other concubine(s) settle east of the Promised Land. Abraham dies at the advanced age of 175 years, and his sons bury him in the Machpelah cave, beside Sarah. Moses brings this brief section to a close by pointing out that God begins to bless Isaac in the same way that He blessed Abraham.

The Descendants of Abraham Through Hagar

As He had promised, God blesses Ishmael for Abraham's sake. He fathers 12 sons, all of them tribal leaders who rise to prominence in Sinai, *"from Havilah to Shur, which is opposite Egypt"* (25:18). Ishmael's sons are hostile toward one another, and their lives are marked by violence and warfare.

Abraham's Birthright Conveyed to Isaac's Twins

Genesis now comes to a major turning point: Abraham's life is over and a new era is beginning. Isaac's story serves primarily as the bridge between Abraham and Jacob.

Isaac soon finds that his wife is barren. Recognizing that *Yahweh* is the one who opens and closes the womb, Isaac prays for Rebekah. He has to wait 20 years for his first child to arrive. The wait must have been difficult for Rebekah as well. When the pregnancy finally happens, she realizes that her pregnancy is not normal. The life inside her is unusually active. She goes to *"inquire of the LORD"* regarding the cause. Rebekah may not have been surprised to learn that she was bearing twins. The youngsters would grow up to be the heads of two distinct nations that would not live in harmony. One family group would be more powerful, and the dominant family would be that of the younger son: *"When Rebecca had conceived ... though they were not yet born and had done nothing either good or bad—in order that God's purpose of election might continue, not because of works but because of Him who calls—she was told, 'The older will serve the younger'"* (Romans 9:10-12). When the twins are born, the first son to arrive is named *Esau*, which means *hairy*. Jacob, the younger son, enters the world grasping Esau's heel. This is prophetic, suggesting that the boys would be competitive. *Jacob* means *supplanter* (Genesis 27:36) and is related to the Hebrew word for *heel*.

Two significant themes in Genesis find their most important expression in Isaac and Jacob. The first is "divine reversals." Here an older and stronger person is set aside in favor of a younger and weaker one. This begins when the offering of Cain, the elder brother, is set aside in favor of Abel, the younger. Cain's line is rejected while that of younger brother, Seth, forms the ancestry of the coming Redeemer. Then Isaac, the younger brother, receives prominence over his older brother, Ishmael. Later, Rachel will be favored over her older sister, Leah; Joseph will be chosen as the favored son of Jacob; and Judah will be selected in preference to his older brothers. The second theme, the importance of God's sovereign choice, is evident in each case.

Abraham's Birthright Abandoned by the Firstborn

By the time the twins are young adults, Esau is his father's favorite and Jacob is Rebekah's. Next comes a crucial encounter: Jacob is at home, cooking stew when Esau arrives home from *"the field"*—perhaps hunting. The aroma of Jacob's stew appeals to his hearty appetite. *"Quick,"* he insists, *"Let me eat some of that red stew!"* Jacob is willing to satisfy Esau's hunger, but for a steep price. He demands the sale of the birthright that was normally the elder son's inheritance. Esau readily agrees. The writer accurately summarizes: *"Thus Esau despised his birthright."*

Think about being "set aside." Think about being passed over at work and the promotion you expected to get being given to someone else. Think about having a sibling who is prettier, or more handsome, or smarter than you. Think about someone else getting all the praise when you did most of the work. Think about God making a sovereign choice to use someone other than you. As a child it hurts when you get chosen last for a team on the playground. Later in the story we will see how Esau felt and responded to being set aside. Just as God has work for each of us to do, He has a position for each of us to hold, a role for each of us to play. When we can accept God's choices as right for us, we will experience peace, because we will be able to say with Paul, *"I have learned in whatever situation I am to be content"* (Philippians 4:11).

The author of Hebrews advises, *"[See] that no one is sexually immoral or unholy like Esau, who sold his birthright for a single meal. For you know that afterward, when he desired to inherit the blessing, he was rejected"* (Hebrews 12:16-17). Although he was born into a family blessed by God, Esau is willing to toss aside his future rewards for the sake of earthly comfort and short-term benefits. The writer of Hebrews presses the point by noting our awesome spiritual birthright: *"Therefore let us be grateful for receiving a kingdom that cannot be shaken, and thus let us offer to God acceptable worship, with reverence and awe"* (Hebrews 12:28-29).

Personalize this lesson.

☑ Esau was living for instant gratification—what the apostle Paul would call *"unspiritual"* or *"fleshly"* (Colossians 2:18, NKJV). He came home tired and hungry, smelled the delicious aroma of stew, and demanded food—now! Jacob, who had doubtless been trying to figure a way to "help" God keep His promise that he would rule over his older brother, seized this opportunity to buy Esau's birthright. That birthright conveyed a double portion of inheritance of Isaac's great wealth. More importantly, it included the covenant promise to Abraham that through his bloodline all people on earth would be blessed. Esau certainly had his value system skewed!

Each day we face choices between a "quick fix" for our temporal appetites or patiently pursuing eternal goals. Are you starving for *"red stew,"* or are you willing to let your stomach growl (figuratively or literally) as you pursue the eternal rewards of an eternal relationship with the Lord? Don't wait; consider now how you will choose when you face an Esau-like choice between the temporal and the eternal.

God Confirms the Covenant
Genesis 26

Memorize God's Word: Galatians 3:29.

❖ Genesis 26:1-11—God Confirms the Line of the Covenant

NOTE: Abimelech is probably a title of Philistine kings, rather than the name of a person, so this Abimelech is most likely a son or grandson of Abraham's Abimelech.

1. For what purposes does God appear to Isaac in this passage?

2. What specific promises of the Abrahamic covenant will be passed down to Isaac?

3. What commentary on Abraham's life does God give after reconfirming the oath He had sworn to Isaac's father?

4. Even with God's promises still ringing in his ears, what sinful actions does Isaac choose to take in this passage?

5. a. What harmful effects did this incident have on others?

_____

_____

    b. What harmful effects can our sins have on others?

_____

_____

❖ Genesis 26:12-25—God Blesses the Son of the Covenant

6. What tangible evidence of God blessing Isaac does the passage describe?

_____

_____

7. Even at this early stage of their history, what reaction does this evidence of God's blessing on His chosen people provoke among others?

_____

_____

_____

8. This passage also records a positive example of Isaac following in his father's footsteps. What is it? (See also Genesis 12:8.)

_____

_____

_____

❖ Genesis 26:26-33—God Establishes Isaac in the Land of the Covenant

9. Why do Abimelech and his top officials pay a visit to Isaac in Beersheba?

_____

_____

10. How does Isaac respond to their proposal?

_____

_____

11. God blessed Isaac with economic prosperity. In what other ways can God bless a believer's life?

_____

_____

12. What do these passages tell us to do when unbelievers ask us about God's blessings?

   a. Colossians 4:5-6_____

   _____

   b. 1 Peter 3:15-16 _____

   _____

13. What answer are you prepared to give when others ask why you have hope in the midst of difficulty or sorrow?

_____

_____

❖ Genesis 26:34-35—Esau Rejects the Value of the Covenant

14. a. What was the first indication of Esau's disregard for the value of his birthright and God's covenant? (See Genesis 25:27-34.)

   _____

   _____

   b. What further indication of his rejection of God's covenant is seen here? (Compare Esau's attitude with Abraham's in Genesis 24:3.)

   _____

   _____

15. Why do you think this incident caused his parents so much grief?

   _____

   _____

16. What commands do the following Scriptures give to believers who want to marry?

   a.   1 Corinthians 7:39 _____

   _____

   b.   2 Corinthians 6:14-16 _____

   _____

17. Do you think our heavenly Father cares whom we choose as a spouse or as friends? Why?

   _____

   _____

   _____

Apply what you have learned. *"When a man's ways please the Lord, He makes even his enemies to be at peace with him"* (Proverbs 16:7). Acting as a true patriarch, Isaac settles down in the land as instructed by God, then graciously moves away and digs new wells when jealous Philistines stop up the old ones. When the Lord appears to him, he immediately sets up an altar and worships. Even the Philistines recognize God's blessing on him and seek him out, asking for a peace treaty. Graciously, he serves a feast and the sides declare peace. That same day, Isaac's servants race in with news: *"We have found water"* (26:32). God not only arranges for Isaac's enemies to live at peace with him, but provides the water Isaac needs. Let's choose to live lives pleasing to the Lord. To what part of your world might God be calling you to bring peace? Who knows, God may choose to pour out His blessings on your peacemaking efforts, too.

God Confirms the Covenant
Genesis 26

Genesis 26 introduces us to Isaac, the second patriarch. This chapter reveals that spiritual growth cannot be inherited; God must shape lives with each new generation. Like his father, Abraham, Isaac stumbles at the beginning, but he learns that *Yahweh's* faithfulness is independent of his own. God shows in this section that He will take care of Isaac and help him become a blessing to others, whether or not Isaac merits such benefits.

God Protects the Line of the Covenant

Here God begins to draw Isaac to Himself, and—as with his father—He starts by allowing a famine to reach the patriarch's home area. If Isaac immediately headed for Egypt to escape it, the most direct route would take him through Gerar, where, years earlier, a king named Abimelech had taken Sarah into his harem and had rebuked Abraham for the deception that caused him severe problems. Now, another Abimelech does the same with Rebekah and eventually rebukes Isaac for his duplicity. (These Abimelechs were almost certainly not the same individual. *Abimelech*, which means *my father is king*, is a title.)

During the famine, God appears to Isaac and warns him against going to Egypt. Instead, he should dwell in the region controlled by Abimelech, where God will bless him. The area under Abimelech's authority is inside the land promised to Abraham. God renews the promises to Isaac and his descendants. As a result of God's blessing, all nations will be blessed through Isaac and his offspring—a promise that has been fulfilled through the coming of Isaac's descendant, the Savior, Jesus Christ.

Although Isaac obeys God by staying in Gerar, he soon stumbles—as his father did—by not trusting God to protect him. Rebekah, a beautiful woman, attracts a great deal of attention from the local men. Fearful of losing his life if he admits that Rebekah is his wife, Isaac claims that she is his sister.

Eventually the truth emerges. Abimelech then holds Isaac accountable for his deception. Like his father, this patriarch finds himself in the embarrassing position of receiving a moral rebuke from a man with a limited knowledge of *Yahweh*. Abimelech orders his people to leave Isaac and Rebekah alone.

God Blesses Isaac and Increases Him

A recurring pattern in Genesis is to find a patriarch misbehaving in one paragraph and then to find a reference to his prospering in the next. After the episode at Gerar, Isaac turns to farming. In the following year he reaps an enormous crop. The explanation is simply, *"The LORD blessed him"* (26:12). God does not wait until His people have gained spiritual maturity before He blesses them—He does so whenever He pleases.

Think about presuming on the goodness of God. Isaac surely knew his material blessings were not God's stamp of approval on his lying to Abimelech. It is easy to assume that God doesn't notice or care when we experience no *immediate* penalty for our unacceptable behavior. God is patient, but He is also just. There will be a day of reckoning, so we must keep short accounts with Him. He will forgive our sins and cleanse us from all unrighteousness if we confess. We must not presume we have gotten away with something because we haven't paid a price yet.

Isaac's wealth increases steadily thereafter. His community becomes so large with flocks, herds, and servants that the Philistines around Gerar envy him. They see him as a threat and stop up the wells that Abraham's servants had dug long before, pushing Isaac farther away from water sources. Abimelech urges Isaac, *"Go away from us, for you are much mightier than we"* (26:16). Isaac moves a short distance away and re-digs the wells that had been filled in. When his servants open a brand-new well, the locals claim even this as their own. Isaac moves farther away and digs another well, but the herdsmen of Gerar argue over the new one. That leads Isaac to name it *Sitnah, enmity.* (The Hebrew root of this term appears also in the name *Satan, adversary.*) Isaac moves again and digs a third well, which is not contested. Assuming that it is only a matter of time until the Philistines will covet his new campsite and well, he returns to his old camp at Beersheba.

That very night, as Isaac wonders if he will ever be safe in the Promised Land, *Yahweh* appears to him. God confirms His covenant and encourages the patriarch to trust Him. Isaac commemorates the occasion by building an altar in Beersheba and calling on the name of *Yahweh* in worship. Soon Abimelech and his advisers appear at Isaac's tent. The leaders of the city recognize that God's hand is upon Isaac, which makes him a threat. They have come to Beersheba to establish a treaty with Isaac and his company. They are clearly afraid of the patriarch's family, because God's blessing is so manifestly his. Isaac celebrates the occasion by providing a generous feast, and the Philistines return to Gerar.

The closing verses of the chapter provide a dramatic contrast to this happy picture. Esau is now 40 years old; his father Isaac was 40 when Abraham's servant brought Rebekah to be his bride. As two worshipers of *Yahweh*, they were to pass God's covenant to a new generation. Esau has no such concerns. Instead of marrying a follower of the living God, Esau chooses to marry two Hittite women, who would not have shared the patriarch's convictions. As a result, *"they made life bitter for Isaac and Rebekah"* (26:35). Esau cares little for the spiritual side of life and even less for his birthright. He proves himself unworthy of the blessing that Jacob will soon steal from him.

Personalize this lesson.

☑ How many grieving parents are reading these words? Many of us have anguished over wrong choices our children have made. And we ask ourselves, "Where did I go wrong?" Isaac's twin sons had different hearts. Heartbroken parents, hear this clearly: Children make choices, and choices have consequences. We can only train, guide, and discipline. We do the best we can with the knowledge we have at the time, and we must never stop praying! Our job as parents is to try to turn our children's hearts toward God, knowing that some hearts turn toward Him, and others turn away. Of course, we feel the pain. But a peaceful heart is a powerful testimony to the world around us that God is sustaining us in the midst of a difficult situation. Let your pain teach you how to trust God more and pray that the supernatural peace you have will point others to the Lord, who gives you peace in all circumstances.

God Reaches Out to Jacob
Genesis 27–28

❖ Genesis 27:1-29—Hijacking the Blessing

1. According to custom and human law, which of Isaac's sons was entitled to the birthright and blessing? Which son had God already chosen to inherit the covenant? (See Genesis 25:22-23.)

   _____

   _____

   _____

2. a. What had this son done to deserve the blessing? And what does this tell us about God? (See also Psalm 115:3; Romans 9:11-18.)

   _____

   _____

   b. Why is it important for us to keep this principle in mind? (See Ephesians 2:8-9; Titus 3:5.)

   _____

   _____

   _____

3. What previous indications of his indifference to his birthright have we seen in Esau? (See Genesis 25:29-34; 26:34-35.)

   _____

   _____

   _____

4. Considering Genesis 25:28; 26:7-8; and 27:1-25, what do you think was the atmosphere in Isaac and Rebekah's home?

_____

_____

_____

5. What warnings about showing favoritism can we glean from this unfortunate situation?

_____

_____

6. What scheme does Isaac initiate in this passage? How do Rebekah and Jacob thwart it?

_____

_____

_____

7. Why do you think Isaac was ready to ignore God's revealed will in this situation?

_____

_____

❖ Genesis 27:30-41—Losing the Blessing

8. What is the outcome of Rebekah and Jacob's deceitful plan?

_____

_____

9. a. How does Esau react when he learns what has happened?

_____

_____

b. What "spin" does he put on his earlier indifference to the birthright? (See also Genesis 25:29-34.)

_____

_____

10. How would you summarize Isaac's prophecy concerning each of his sons (27:28-29, 39-40)?

   a. Jacob _____

      _____

   b. Esau _____

      _____

11. What future revenge does Esau decide to take at this point?

    _____

    _____

❖ Genesis 27:42-28:9—Protecting the Heir

12. How does Rebekah continue to manipulate both Isaac and Jacob in her scheme to save Jacob's life?

    _____

    _____

    _____

13. In his belated sense of responsibility for his family and the covenant, what steps does Isaac take to repair the damage?

    _____

    _____

14. How do you see God working out His preordained purposes in this story, in spite of the sinners He has to work with?

    _____

    _____

❖ Genesis 28:10-22—Confirming the Blessing

15. How would you describe Jacob's encounter with God on his journey to Haran? What message was God conveying to Jacob through this encounter?

    _____

    _____

16. Aside from restating the terms of the covenant to Jacob, what personal promises does God give him? Were any of these promises conditional?

_____

_____

_____

17. What do you think Jacob's previous relationship with God had been? How is it changed by this experience?

_____

_____

18. Can you recall a particular time when God revealed Himself, His will, or His love to you in a special way? If so, please share how this experience transformed your relationship with Him.

_____

_____

_____

Apply what you have learned. Jacob's vow makes an important point about spiritual immaturity. God has appeared to Jacob and renewed the covenant promises. But he clearly does not understand what it means to trust God. Notice the conditions he places on God: God must be with him and watch over him, providing food, clothing, and a safe journey. If God complies, *then* Jacob will call Him his God, dedicate that spot to Him, and tithe. Later he will learn that he is not in a position to bargain with God. Nor are we! Jacob can only see his needs for the immediate journey. What do your prayers reveal about your spiritual maturity? Where do you pray with "strings attached"? Commit your situation to God and ask Him for faith to trust Him with it.

God Reaches Out to Jacob
Genesis 27–28

In Genesis 27–28 Isaac is seen as elderly, feeble, and blind. Unfortunately, his blindness also extends to spiritual matters. He is determined to oppose God's earlier declaration giving preeminence to Jacob. God folds Rebekah and Isaac's schemes into His historical purpose and grants Jacob the blessing. Jacob finds the blessing easier to gain than to keep, however, for Esau soon makes plans to kill him. Jacob leaves for Haran—fleeing for his life. On the journey he meets the God of his fathers.

Manipulating the Blessing

When Esau sold his birthright to Jacob, he must have felt secure, assuming that his father would have the final say about distributing the family assets and *Yahweh's* promises. Indeed, when Isaac is 137 years old and in failing health, he asks Esau to prepare a special meal, after which he will formally convey to his firstborn the covenant promises *Yahweh* had made to Abraham.

Think about self-centered priorities. Isaac plans to enjoy a tasty meal of wild game and then have a secret ceremony to give Esau the blessing that God has decreed for Jacob. Isaac is determined to oppose God's will. It's good to be mindful about how we prioritize all the wonderful things God has given us to enjoy. They may lead us away from the one who gave them. When preoccupied with earthly cares or pleasures, it is easy to drift away from God and rationalize that His will can be safely ignored. Seeking to know and do God's will is far better than selfishly focusing on this life's pleasures.

Rebekah hears the conversation between Isaac and Esau, so she orders Jacob to help her plan an elaborate deception. She will prepare a tasty meal for the patriarch. Then Jacob, impersonating Esau, will serve the food to his father and thus receive the blessing of the firstborn. To trick Isaac, Jacob will wear Esau's clothes, and goatskin on his hands and neck to imitate his brother's body hair. Jacob presents himself to Isaac as Esau. Blind Isaac is suspicious and cautious; he demands that the "firstborn" come near so that he can feel the garments and skin of the one to be blessed. Finally, Isaac seems content and joyful when he experiences the delightful smell of Esau's clothes. In four brief sentences, he conveys legal title to the blessings of the Abrahamic covenant. These blessings include (1) material prosperity, (2) preference among the nations, (3) preference within his family, and (4) passing God's blessings on to others.

Losing the Blessing

No sooner has this sad charade been concluded than Esau arrives. Instantly, Isaac trembles at the realization that he has been deceived. Just as quickly, he yields to the plan God had declared earlier. He concedes that Jacob has not only received the blessing but will retain the blessing. God has spoken, not only by the prophecy, but also by circumstances. His words crush Esau, who blames Jacob for taking his birthright. In reality, Esau had sold it to him for a bowl of stew, demonstrating just how low his opinion of the birthright truly was.

Esau's attempt to recoup the blessing begins with a question for his father: *"Have you not reserved a blessing for me?"* (27:36). Isaac's reply makes clear that in blessing Jacob, he has been effectively speaking for God. *"I have made him lord over you"* (27:37) is a statement that recognizes God's power behind what has been said. God has not approved deception, but He has integrated the sins of others into His own purpose.

After Esau's weeping and pleadings, Isaac pronounces a blessing on Esau, which does not compromise Jacob's promised blessing. Esau will live in an arid land; his reputation will be for warfare. Eventually, the break between the twins will be embodied in rebellion. Isaac's words are prophetic; years later, Esau's descendants, the Edomites, settle in the rocky terrain of Mount Seir, southeast of the Dead Sea. Esau plans to kill Jacob when Isaac dies.

Preserving the Heir

When Esau speaks about revenge against his brother, Rebekah quickly alerts Jacob to the danger. He is to abandon Canaan and stay a while with her brother Laban. She believes that, in time, Jacob will safely return. Rebekah gives Jacob a cover story for his departure to Haran. Referring to Esau's Hittite wives, Rebekah tells Isaac, *"I loathe my life because of the Hittite women"* (27:46). Isaac agrees that Jacob should seek a wife among the couple's relatives back in Haran, and sends his son north with a stern warning to marry one of Rebekah's nieces. Rebekah will never see Jacob again.

Encounter at Bethel

Jacob knows little of *Yahweh* beyond His reputation. God soon begins to address Jacob's spiritual ignorance during the long trip northward. Stopping at the place where Abram had sojourned long before, Jacob retires for the night. As he sleeps, God appears to him in a dream. Jacob sees a stairway between earth and heaven with *"the LORD"* above it. *Yahweh* speaks to him in the dream, identifying Himself as the God of Abraham and Isaac. He then confirms all the promises of the Abrahamic covenant, adding a vow to bring Jacob back to Canaan, eventually.

Jacob now has direct knowledge of *Yahweh*. He determines that the experience will mark a turning point in his relationship with God. He memorializes the place by setting up the stone upon which he had slept and pouring oil on it. He names it *Bethel, house of God.* Bethel would be an important location throughout the remainder of the Old Testament, with many of Scripture's pivotal events taking place within a few miles of it. Jacob's knowledge of God is still incomplete. Instead of simply bowing before God because of the vision he has seen and recognizing God's greatness, Jacob bargains with *Yahweh*. He will follow *Yahweh* as his God only if He provides faithfully for him during the uncertain time ahead. God will prove Himself to be faithful. The question is, will Jacob?

Personalize this lesson.

Because we are flawed people living in a flawed world, we will make mistakes in our marriages and in our parenting. Genesis puts Isaac's family under the spiritual microscope, so that we can learn from and avoid their mistakes. Mistake number 1: Isaac and Rebekah chose favorites—a recipe for disaster. Mistake number 2: Isaac and Rebekah failed to communicate. Mistake number 3: They did not agree on how to handle their children or their problems. Mistake number 4: They did not discourage the competition and animosity between their sons. Mistake number 5: Most importantly, they did not seek God's wisdom. Are any of their mistakes being played out in your family? Ask God how you can work with Him to restore broken relationships and enable communication to be reestablished. Then follow through on what He shows you.

The Children of Jacob
Genesis 29–30

❖ Genesis 29:1-30—Jacob's Predicament

1. Compare Jacob's arrival in Haran with the arrival of Abraham's servant at the same place almost 100 years earlier (24:10-30). How are the two episodes similar? What key difference do you see in how the two men approached their wife-finding task?

   _____

   _____

   _____

2. How do you see God at work behind the scenes for Jacob?

   _____

   _____

   _____

3. Why do you think Laban received Jacob so warmly?

   _____

   _____

4. When asked, what wages does Jacob ask Laban for?

   _____

5. What happens to Jacob on his wedding night? What do we learn about Laban from this?

   _____

   _____

6. How does this episode illustrate the truth of Galatians 6:7?

    _____

    _____

❖ Genesis 29:31–30:24—Jacob's Children

7. Describe how the statement *"he loved Rachel more than Leah"* (29:30) might have played out in Leah's marriage day-by-day.

    _____

    _____

    _____

8. How does the Lord compensate for Leah's rejection? What does this tell you about God?

    _____

    _____

9. a. How do the names of Leah's first three sons reflect her craving for her husband's affection? (Use your Bible's footnotes.) Do these children fulfill her desires?

    _____

    _____

    _____

    b. How does her fourth son's name show her change of focus?

    _____

    _____

10. a. What causes Rachel's unhappiness? Whom does she blame?

    _____

    _____

    b. How does she try to fix her problem, and with what results?

    _____

    _____

c. What does Leah do that further complicates family relationships?

_____

_____

11. a. What do the names of Jacob's fifth, sixth, seventh, and eighth sons (30:4-13) tell us about these two sisters?

_____

_____

b. How does the name Rachel gives her firstborn son reveal her continued state of discontent?

_____

_____

12. Even though both Leah and Rachel attempt to manipulate their husband's affections in order to have children, who is really in control of this family's growth? Give references.

_____

_____

❖ Genesis 30:25-43—Jacob's Prosperity

13. Why does Jacob want to leave?

_____

_____

14. Why does Laban want Jacob to stay?

_____

_____

15. a. When Laban refuses to give Jacob permission to leave, what counter offer does Jacob make?

_____

_____

b. What new strategy does Laban initiate "before the ink has time to dry" on their agreement?

_____

_____

c. How does Jacob also try to improve his position? Does it work? Why or why not? (See also Genesis 31:42.)

_____

_____

16. a. How does God use Laban in Jacob's life?

_____

_____

b. How can this encourage you to trust God if you have experienced or if you are experiencing injustice?

_____

_____

Apply what you have learned. Perhaps one of the reasons Jacob had to spend 20 years with Laban was so he could learn that God, not he, was in control. Certainly in the matter of human offspring he came to understand that God alone determines the gift of life (30:2). No matter how much he and Rachel longed for a child, only God could open her womb. Nor did he have any real control over the breeding of his flocks, despite the branches he peeled. Again, God is in control. God drove this point home with a dream. What circumstances do you try to control? How does Jacob's story challenge you? Talk to God about the changes you'd like to make with His help.

The Children of Jacob
Genesis 29–30

The Bible frequently refers to *"the children of Israel."* In this lesson, we see 11 of the children of Jacob—who has yet to receive his new name, *Israel*—enter the world. These sons will form the core of the new nation promised to Abraham and Isaac. Although Jacob has encountered *Yahweh* at Bethel, he does not yet know his God well. Jacob's manipulation of Isaac and Esau for his own ends brings him to Haran. There he meets his uncle Laban, a man whose skill at manipulation exceeds his own. Because of Laban's trickery, Jacob finds himself yoked to a wife he does not love. While the patriarch-in-training mishandles his blessings, God is at work, blessing him until he is the wealthy and imposing head of a large family.

The Trickster Is Tricked

Like Abraham's servant, Jacob arrives at a well in Haran and God guides his steps to Laban's family. Some shepherds point out Laban's daughter, Rachel, and Jacob is so delighted to see her that he kisses her and begins to weep with glad relief. Rachel summons Laban, who warmly greets the son of the sister he had sent to Canaan (Genesis 24). Laban senses that he might be able to use his nephew to gain additional wealth. Jacob may see himself as clever, but his uncle is a cunning man with a set of loose principles that flex according to the advantage he seeks.

Soon Jacob finds himself working for his uncle. Laban begins to hatch a clever plan that will guarantee him a free employee for the next 14 years. Leah, his eldest daughter, is not particularly appealing. Her younger sister Rachel is Jacob's great passion. Jacob agrees to work for seven years if he can marry Rachel, and Laban is happy to comply. Jacob finds that the time flies by because he is near his beloved Rachel.

At last the time comes when Jacob can claim his bride, and they celebrate the wedding feast. In the morning, however, he discovers that Leah is beside him, not Rachel. When Jacob demands an explanation, Laban replies that he can have Rachel as well—but it is the family's custom to marry off the older daughter first. Jacob must allow Leah the dignity of a week's wedding celebration; then he may marry Rachel. Of course, he will have to serve another seven years.

The Blessing Mishandled

God finds Jacob's treatment of Leah offensive, so He blesses her with an early pregnancy. Rachel, however, is barren. Leah names her firstborn *Reuben*, meaning, *See! A son!* The name reflects her belief that God has seen her misery from lacking her husband's affection. She believes this son will stir Jacob to give her the love she desires. Soon she is pregnant again, and a second son arrives, whom she names *Simeon*, meaning *hearing*—a testimony of faith to God's compensation for her unloved condition. She again gives birth to a son and names him *Levi*, meaning *attached, joined*. Her fourth son is *Judah*, *praise*. She resolves not to pine away for Jacob but instead to praise the Lord.

Watching her sister present Jacob with four fine sons, Rachel's jealousy grows and she lashes out at Jacob, demanding that he give her children. Clearly, Jacob's fertility is not the problem. Rachel is so desperate that she gives her maidservant to her husband; any children born from the union would make her (legally, at least) a mother. When Bilhah becomes pregnant, Rachel feels vindicated. She names the boy *Dan*, meaning *judgment, vindication*. This arrangement is continued, and Bilhah has a second son whom Rachel names *Naphtali—wrestlings, struggles*. Leah adopts Rachel's strategy and offers Jacob her maid Zilpah, who bears him two sons, *Gad*, meaning *luck*, and *Asher*, meaning *happy*.

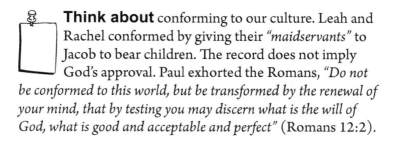

Think about conforming to our culture. Leah and Rachel conformed by giving their *"maidservants"* to Jacob to bear children. The record does not imply God's approval. Paul exhorted the Romans, *"Do not be conformed to this world, but be transformed by the renewal of your mind, that by testing you may discern what is the will of God, what is good and acceptable and perfect"* (Romans 12:2).

A lot goes on around us that does not have God's approval, so weigh your decisions carefully. *"Don't let the world around you squeeze you into its own mold"* (Romans 12:2, PH).

Jacob is now the father of eight sons. When Reuben harvests some mandrake plants—which many believed to be an aphrodisiac—and brings them to Leah, Rachel asks for them. In payment, Rachel grants Leah the privilege of having Jacob spend the night with her. Although Rachel possesses the mandrakes, Leah becomes pregnant. Leah names her new son *Issachar,* meaning *wages,* since she had "hired" his father. Then Leah conceives again and names her sixth son *Zebulon,* which may mean *honor* or *dwelling,* because she seems to hope that bearing Jacob so many sons will encourage him to leave Rachel's tent and move in with her. Her last child is a girl, *Dinah.* After 10 sons and one daughter are born to her husband's other wives, God has compassion on Rachel; she becomes pregnant and delivers a son, whom she names *Joseph,* meaning *may* [the Lord] *add.*

Blessing in Spite of Manipulation

With 20 years of labor behind him, Jacob at last decides to return to Canaan. Laban, however, is not ready to part with him and invites Jacob to name his price for staying in Paddan Aram. Laban claims to have learned by divination that his prosperity is a consequence of Jacob's presence. Scripture condemns this occult practice (Leviticus 19:26; Deuteronomy 18:10-11). Laban's participation in it displays his limited commitment to *Yahweh.*

Jacob agrees to stay, accepting as his wages the speckled and spotted sheep and goats of Laban's flocks. Immediately Laban carefully and dishonestly segregates these animals from the flock, removing them from Jacob's access. Jacob then attempts to increase the spotted animals through a strange manipulation. But God—with no help from tree limbs—increases the speckled animals and blesses Jacob, a fact he will later acknowledge.

Personalize this lesson.

✓ Jacob's life illustrates how God blesses and uses people even when that blessing is unearned and undeserved. Despite all his flaws, God gave Jacob 11 sons, a daughter, and great wealth. Through his bloodline, Messiah would be born. Do you ever look at someone in an effective ministry and ask yourself, "How would God use *her*?" Or "Does God realize what *he* has done?" Do we look at *ourselves* and ask the same questions? Obviously, God is not looking for perfection, but availability. God uses whom He chooses. Let's be grateful He can use imperfect people. How does Jacob's story encourage you?

God Protects Jacob
Genesis 31

Memorize God's Word: Genesis 31:16b.

❖ Genesis 31:1-16—Jacob's Complaint

1. Why does Jacob want to return to Canaan and how does God confirm that desire?

   _____

   _____

2. How do Leah and Rachel respond to Jacob's grievances?

   _____

   _____

3. Has God ever used your discontentment with circumstances in order to prompt you to move where He wanted you to go?

   _____

   _____

❖ Genesis 31:17-35—Laban's Pursuit

4. Why do you think Jacob and his family left in secret?

   _____

5. What emotion often motivated Jacob's actions? (See also Genesis 31:31 and 32:7, 11.)

   _____

   _____

6. If this emotion is a motivating factor in your life, how could Psalm 56:3-4 help you overcome it?

_____

_____

7. Jacob's decision to leave secretly allows Laban to play the role of the injured party. What accusations does Laban voice?

_____

_____

_____

8. What does Rachel's behavior at the time of their departure, and later when Laban arrives, reveal about her spiritual maturity?

_____

_____

9. What real threat to this family does Laban's arrival present?

_____

_____

10. What had God already done to protect Jacob and his family from Laban?

_____

_____

11. What does the Lord's protection of Jacob and his family tell you about God in view of His promise in Genesis 28:15?

_____

_____

12. Has God ever protected you, even when you were partly or wholly responsible for your predicament? How?

_____

_____

_____

❖ Genesis 31:36-42—Jacob's Rebuke

13. Jacob's anger at Laban provokes him to recite a long list of his grievances. Of what two wrongs does he accuse him?

_____

_____

14. To whom does Jacob give credit for the fact that he has prospered in spite of Laban's schemes?

_____

15. What dangers to a family resulting from unresolved differences do you see in this passage?

_____

_____

16. What warnings about unresolved differences between Christians does Jesus give in Matthew 5:21-26?

_____

_____

17. According to Jesus, in Matthew 18:15-35, what are your responsibilities if you are the one who has been wronged?

_____

_____

❖ Genesis 31:43-55—The Pillars at Mizpah

18. How does Laban answer Jacob? Is he telling the truth?

_____

_____

19. How does Laban propose that he and Jacob resolve their enmity?

_____

_____

20. Are the covenant and the pillars they erect intended to be a blessing or a safeguard against a threat? Explain your answer.

_____

_____

21. Who does Laban call as his witness should Jacob violate the terms of their agreement?

_____

_____

22. How is the covenant sealed and the potential threat to the heir of the Abrahamic covenant ended?

_____

_____

23. What lessons have you learned from Jacob's experiences with Laban?

_____

_____

Apply what you have learned. The Mizpah blessing, *"The LORD watch between you and me, when we are out of one another's sight"* (31:49), is not a warm benediction. Rather, Laban was (rather hypocritically, for he had been far from an ideal father) warning Jacob to treat his daughters properly because God would be watching. Nevertheless, declaring God to be at the center of our family squabbles can bring peace, even if one or both parties have less than ideal motives. Let the Lord be the witness who sees you apply godly love: *"Love is patient and kind; love does not envy or boast; it is not arrogant or rude. ... Love bears all things, believes all things, hopes all things, endures all things"* (1 Corinthians 13:4-8). As you go through the rest of this week, keep in mind that the Lord is witness to all your relational interactions.

Lesson 21 Commentary

God Protects Jacob
Genesis 31

Genesis 30 described how God allowed Jacob's flocks to increase.
Genesis 31 shows that the patriarch sees God at work, carefully
protecting him from his father-in-law's predatory intentions. Jacob will
have to fulfill the vow he made at Bethel, for God has done exactly as
he asked. Jacob obeys God, and God protects him. Jacob concludes
that meeting Esau poses less danger than remaining near Laban and his
persistent crookedness. Jacob departs from his father-in-law secretly,
taking wives, children, and flocks. Though Laban eventually overtakes
him, God protects Jacob by rebuking Laban in a dream. The two families
edgily agree on parting terms, and Jacob is at last free of his uncle—but
now he must face his brother.

Jacob's Complaint

Jacob had arrived in Paddan Aram penniless, while Laban was wealthy;
now Jacob is rich, and Laban's wealth is declining. Laban and his sons
become hostile toward Jacob. *Yahweh* tells Jacob to return to Canaan.

Jacob is about to leave, knowing that Laban will disapprove. Jacob
calls his wives out into the fields, suggesting that he thinks some of the
servants in his camp are Laban's spies. He gives his reason for leaving
Paddan Aram: he has given honest labor, but Laban is unwilling to see
him prosper. God could have increased Jacob's wealth while adding to
Laban's also, but instead, *"God has taken away the livestock of your father
and given them to me"* (31:9). Jacob's suspicions have been confirmed
by a dream. Rachel and Leah have agreed on very little in the last 13
years, but they agree about leaving Haran. They, too, feel estranged
from Laban. Their father has excluded them from his estate. As far as
Leah and Rachel are concerned, God has been displaying nothing less

than simple justice. They encourage Jacob to follow God's directive and return to Canaan.

Laban's Pursuit

Jacob and his family leave stealthily. Rachel steals her father's household gods (Hebrew, *teraphim*). These teraphim were small idols typically placed in niches in private homes. Rachel may have felt that her theft was justified, because her father had denied her inheritance rights. However, she might simply be taking revenge for her father's rejection.

God is not entirely pleased with the manner of Jacob's leaving, although the patriarch is following a divine directive. The passage implies that Jacob's departure is nothing less than a deception. The same God who had supported him through 20 years in Laban's employment could protect him and his family as they departed. Instead of attempting to leave on good terms, Jacob flees to Gilead, east of the Jordan River. Apparently he plans to stay there for a time and investigate the matter of Esau's hostility before crossing the Jordan. Now, however, instead of having one powerful enemy, he has two.

Think about doing God's will God's way. Jacob had a great advantage: God clearly told him what He wanted him to do. Genesis 31:3 says, *"Then the LORD said to Jacob."* Jacob obeyed, but he fell back on his old way of doing things. Verse 20 says, *"Jacob tricked Laban."* God wants us to do His will His way, even if the way we have figured out seems safer and easier. He wants us to stop scheming and start trusting. We are to ask Him not just what to do, but how to do it. He promised the people of Israel that if they cried out to Him for help, He would answer them and give them clear direction: *"Your ears shall hear a word behind you, saying, "This is the way, walk in it," when you turn to the right or when you turn to the left"* (Isaiah 30:21). Try crying out to Him about what He wants you to do, and how He wants you to do it!

Laban hears of Jacob's deception two days after his departure. Seven days later he overtakes Jacob's company in the hill country of Gilead. God protects Jacob by appearing to Laban in a dream in which He sternly warns Laban not to *"say anything to Jacob, either good or bad"* (31:29). But Laban cannot resist rebuking Jacob. He insists that he would have sent Jacob away with a feast and a celebration had he known the patriarch's intent. He acknowledges that God has warned him against harming Jacob. His primary complaint, however, is that Jacob has stolen his gods. At his core, Laban is an idolater. Not knowing about Rachel's theft, Jacob promises to punish the offender and to return any of Laban's property that might be found in his encampment. Rachel deceives her father by hiding the teraphs inside her camel's saddle and then lying to him. Thus Laban, the con artist, is fleeced by his own daughter.

The Pillars of Mizpah

Laban's pursuit and accusations provoke Jacob to charge him with dishonesty. Jacob censures Laban for his crooked treatment of his own family. Jacob has given Laban 20 years of honest labor, but apart from God's intervention, he would be leaving Haran penniless. Jacob can testify to *Yahweh's* greatness and sustaining power. The dream that Laban experienced, Jacob insists, is nothing less than a rebuke from heaven itself. Characteristically, Laban remains unrepentant, and even his own daughters regard his behavior as contemptible.

God has restricted Laban from reprisals, so all that remains is to establish a covenant that will define the families' future relationship. The parties to the new treaty do not trust each other, so this relationship will be uneasy. The families erect two stone memorial pillars to serve, in effect, as border markers between their respective domains. Jacob will not travel east of the pillars, and Laban will not travel west of them. The two men cannot even agree on names for the pillars. Each names his marker in his own tongue. The same monuments were also called—later, perhaps— *Mizpah*, a Hebrew word meaning *watchtower*. Jacob and Laban seal the ritual by sharing a common meal.

Personalize this lesson.

 In order to get to his uncle's home, Jacob left his own home and headed north. It was a long, difficult journey, past the Dead Sea and across a large stretch of desert. There was no guarantee of food and water, and there was the constant danger of bandits as he traveled alone. But something astounding happened on the journey. God appeared to him, and Jacob made a vow: If God would take care of him and enable him to *"return safely to my father's house, then the LORD shall be my God"* (28:21).

Jacob spent 20 years in the increasingly hostile environment of Laban's home and then—with a large contingent of livestock, servants, women, and children—he traveled back toward his home country. He originally fled from an angry brother; now he flees an angry uncle, knowing his brother is still in the home territory. During those 20 years, God was transforming Jacob. At first, he made his own decisions and just called on God in emergencies, but in chapter 31 we see Jacob invoking God eight times! God has blessed and cared for him. Jacob finally understands that success is possible only because of what God does on our behalf. How does this story encourage you to believe God will watch over you, your household, and your material possessions?

Wrestling With God
Genesis 32–33

Memorize God's Word: Psalm 20:1.

❖ Genesis 32:1-21—Jacob Prepares to Meet Esau

1. a. Why do you think the Lord sends His angels to Jacob at this particular time?

   _____

   _____

   b. What can we learn about God from this?

   _____

   _____

   _____

2. a. What effect does Jacob hope the message he sends to his brother will have?

   _____

   _____

   b. What report does his messenger bring back?

   _____

   _____

   c. What is Jacob's twofold reaction to this message?

   _____

   _____

   _____

3. What can we learn about Jacob from this prayer?

    _____

    _____

4. How has Jacob changed in the 20 years he's been away from
    Canaan?

    _____

    _____

5. a. In spite of his experiences with God, what motivating
        emotion still controls his life?

        _____

        _____

    b. What makes this emotion inconsistent with faith?

        _____

        _____

    c. Consider any areas in your life in which you still struggle
        with this emotion. What could you begin to do today to
        break its hold on your life? (See Psalm 56:3-4; Isaiah 41:10;
        Philippians 4:6-7.)

        _____

        _____

❖ Genesis 32:22-32—Jacob Wrestles With God

6. What happens to Jacob after he sends his family across the
    Jabbok River? With whom does he struggle that night? (See also
    Hosea 12:3-5.)

    _____

    _____

7. a. Names almost always signify character in Scripture. What
        did the name *Jacob* mean? (See Genesis 25:26; 27:36.)

        _____

        _____

b. What new name does God give him at this time? What is its meaning?

_____

_____

❖ Genesis 33:1-20—Jacob Meets Esau

8. a. Twenty years with Laban and various encounters with God have changed Jacob, but old ways and habits die hard. How does Jacob react when he sees Esau and his entourage approaching? In a word, what motivates him to adopt such a strategy?

_____

_____

_____

b. Does his strategy prove necessary? Why or why not?

_____

_____

_____

9. Under what circumstances had these brothers last seen each other? (See Genesis 27:41-45.)

_____

_____

10. How does Jacob approach Esau? When they meet, what does he call Esau, and what does he call himself?

_____

_____

11. How is this exchange ironic in light of the birthright Jacob had "stolen" from Esau many years earlier? (See Genesis 27:29, 39-40.)

_____

_____

_____

12. While no actual admission of guilt is recorded, what message does this exchange send?

_____

_____

13. Why do you think Esau responds as he does to his brother's efforts toward reconciliation?

_____

_____

14. How does the outcome of this encounter illustrate the principle of 1 Peter 5:5-6?

_____

_____

15. How are the actions of both of these men a model of repentance and reconciliation?

_____

_____

Apply what you have learned. Reconciliation requires a person to admit wrongdoing against another and the other to accept the apology. Only when Jacob finally understood submission to his God could he then humbly bow (Genesis 33:3) before the brother he had wronged. The Bible does not record their actual words of apology, but the actions of both men indicate changed hearts. When you have settled the matter with God, He will enable you to settle it with the one you have wronged. Do you have any strained relationships? What is God leading you to do in order to move toward reconciliation? Ask Him for the grace, humility, and courage to take those first steps.

Wrestling With God
Genesis 32–33

No sooner is Jacob free of Laban's dishonesty than he finds himself preparing to meet a military force headed by a man with a grudge. Just as God's appearance encouraged him before his departure from Laban, now angelic messengers encourage him on the eve of his meeting with Esau. He understands that God has not abandoned him, but circumstances make him wary. Has Esau forgiven him? Has his brother assembled the large force to destroy him and his family? These questions linger until God wrestles with Jacob, and the patriarch emerges from the encounter with a new attitude. Jacob will limp for the remainder of his days, but he now sees the limits of self-reliance.

Jacob Prepares to Meet Esau

After Laban's departure, Jacob heads toward the Jordan River. Before he crosses, God sends angels to meet him. He recognizes their appearance as a sign of God's protection, a guarantee that he will survive the encounter with Esau and live to see God's promises fulfilled. It also serves as a subtle reminder of the vow he made at Bethel. The patriarch considers the location to be worthy of a new name: *Mahanaim* (*Two Camps*, or *Twin Camps*).

Jacob seeks a genuine reconciliation with his brother and makes a series of goodwill gestures. His messengers inform Esau that he has become a wealthy man. They return with frightening news: Jacob's older brother is approaching with an entourage of 400 men. This causes Jacob to be *"greatly afraid and distressed"* (32:7). He divides his family and possessions into two companies. If one is attacked, perhaps the other can get away. When he left the land years before, he knew *Yahweh* mostly by reputation. As he returns, he brings *Yahweh's* blessings with him. He had possessed nothing when he departed. Even after years of Laban's dishonesty, he is returning a rich man, which could be attributed only to God. He prays for God's protection.

Jacob Meets God

Jacob decides to sweeten their meeting by sending his brother lavish gifts of livestock, giving a hint of the magnitude of his wealth. To maximize the impact of his 550-animal gift, he segregates the animals into herds so he can stagger their arrivals at Esau's camp. Esau could hardly fail to be impressed with his brother's humble generosity and with the size of his estate.

Jacob sends his wives and maidservants ahead during the middle of the night. He finds himself alone at Mahanaim. Yet he is not alone. Verse 24 says *"a man"* wrestles with him throughout the night. This "man" is none other than the Lord Himself. As so often in Genesis, His glory is veiled. In verse 25 He seems unable to overpower Jacob and insists that their wrestling cease. Yet with merely a touch, He dislocates Jacob's hip joint, demonstrating that He could overpower Jacob at any time. Jacob concludes that his opponent is the One upon whom his whole life depends. God is teaching him that the true struggle of his life is with Him rather than with men.

Jacob seems to understand the message, for he insists that the Visitor bless him before leaving. *"The man"* complies by changing Jacob's name. The patriarch has been known as *Jacob,* the *deceiver.* Henceforth, others will call him *Israel* (*He struggles with God*). He is a changed man, recognizing that he has survived a rare close encounter with God Himself. He is altered physically as well, for the *"man's"* touch will cause him to limp throughout his life. He renames the place *Peniel,* meaning *the face of God.*

Think about sharing with others when God blesses us. As a near-stampede of his animals entered Esau's camp, Jacob told his brother, *"Please accept my blessing … because God has dealt graciously with me, and because I have enough"* (Genesis 33:11). Jacob responded to God's goodness to him by inviting his brother to take part in his prosperity. God has given His good gifts to each of us—time, talents, resources. How can you, like Jacob, multiply what God has given you by passing it on to others?

___

Jacob Meets Esau

No sooner has *"the man"* departed than Esau arrives. Jacob concludes that the 400 men must be a military force. He openly displays a preference for Rachel and Joseph, placing them last in line. He reasons that by the time any conflict reaches the rear, Rachel and Joseph will have escaped. To show his repentant and sincere spirit, he humbles himself by bowing down to Esau seven times.

Esau's men are there to escort them to their new home, not to slaughter them. God honors Jacob's prayer and gives him favor with his brother, who seeks reconciliation. The reunion is emotional for both. Though Esau has come some distance to welcome Jacob and ensure his safety, the patriarch does not seem to want an extended relationship with him. When Esau offers to accompany him as he moves to a permanent camp, Jacob declines. Esau offers to leave guards behind to protect Jacob's family, but Jacob again refuses. Esau heads south to Seir; Jacob turns west and moves to Succoth. There he establishes a semi-permanent settlement by building shelters (Hebrew, *succoth*) for his family and livestock. Jacob stays in this location east of the Jordan for perhaps as long as 10 years.

Afterward, Jacob crosses the Jordan and settles near the town of Shechem. There he purchases a piece of property and settles down. He sets up an altar and worships God in the land that Abraham was told would belong to his children. Jacob calls his shrine *El Elohe Israel* (*God, the God of Israel*). He establishes a testimony among the region's Gentiles that a worshiper of *Yahweh* is now among them, and he takes the first steps toward fulfilling an old vow. Although he has not yet returned to Bethel, he has at least acknowledged before the world that *Yahweh* is indeed his God.

Personalize this lesson.

☑ Jacob physically wrestled with God, who appeared to him in human form. He struggled again as he threw himself on God's mercy in prayer. Prayer is likely the way we wrestle with God, and at times it can feel like a wrestling match. We can learn much from Jacob's prayer. Jacob begins by reminding himself and God of how faithful God had been to his father and grandfather. He is unworthy of God's grace; yet he proceeds to beg for mercy. He bases his rationale solidly on God's promises. Are you wrestling with God over an issue? What promises of God are you depending upon as you work through your situation with God in prayer? Will you "hang in there" with God until He blesses you?

Lesson 23

God Reconfirms the Promises
Genesis 34–36

❖ **Genesis 34—The Defilement of Jacob's Family**

1. Where has Jacob chosen to live at this point in his journey (Genesis 33:18-19)? What location, according to Genesis 31:13; 35:1, might have been a better choice?

    _____

    _____

2. What wrongful act sets the stage for the devastating event recorded in this chapter?

    _____

3. a. What do the young man and his father offer to do in order to compensate for the harm that's been done?

    _____

    b. Why might this offer have seemed advantageous to the men in Jacob's family?

    _____

    _____

4. What emotions motivate Jacob's sons to seek revenge instead?

    _____

5. What motivates the men of Shechem to comply with the demands of Jacob's sons?

    _____

6. Which of Jacob's sons are responsible for the massacre? What part do the others play in this tragic event?

_____

_____

_____

7. What conclusions about Jacob's sons can we draw from this episode?

_____

_____

_____

8. What underlying threat to the covenant emerges in this chapter? (See Genesis 34:9-10.)

_____

_____

9. How can our close relationships influence our walk with Christ?

_____

_____

_____

10. Think of relationships in your life that either encourage you to grow spiritually or hinder your spiritual growth. What can you do to counteract any negative effects the latter might have?

_____

_____

_____

❖ Genesis 35—The Delight of Israel's Future

11. What important step of obedience does Jacob take in response to God's command to return to Bethel?

_____

_____

12. Why was abandoning the false gods (Genesis 35:2, 4) essential for this family who would become heirs of God's covenant? (See also Exodus 20:3-6.)

_____

_____

13. The false gods in Jacob's time were made of metal, stone, or wood. What kinds of false gods are we tempted to worship today?

_____

14. Why does God appear to Jacob at Bethel a second time? (See Genesis 35:9-13.)Why do you think He reconfirmed the change in Jacob's name?

_____

_____

15. What new sorrows come into Jacob's life at this time?

_____

16. What sin toward his father does Reuben commit in Genesis 35:22? What will be the long-term consequences of his action? (See Genesis 49:3-4; 1 Chronicles 5:1.)

_____

17. Can you think of a past action that has had permanent consequences in your own life? How can Romans 8:1, 28-30 encourage you to trust God with those consequences?

_____

_____

❖ Genesis 36—The Departure of Israel's Brother

18. a. How has Esau's choice of wives exposed his indifference toward his family's feelings, and ultimately toward God? (See Genesis 26:34-35; 27:46; 28:6-9.)

_____

_____

  b. What commentary on this man does God give us in Hebrews 12:16?

_____

_____

  c. Can you identify areas today where a Christian's life might reveal indifference toward God and His Word? What could a person do to remedy that?

_____

_____

19. What nation descended from Esau? According to Numbers 20:14-21, how did this nation treat God's chosen people when Israel needed to pass through their land during the Exodus?

_____

_____

20. How does John 3:16-18 express the truth that a "line in the sand" will always divide the people of God from the people who reject Him? Who is that "line"?

_____

_____

Apply what you have learned. Jacob is as much to blame for his sons' brutal sin as they are. Years earlier he had made a vow to God at Bethel, where he should have returned. But he chose to purchase land at Shechem and build an altar there. We cannot worship God as we please! Jacob's altar was in the wrong place. God had to command him to return to Bethel after the atrocities occurred at Shechem. Are you worshiping God in the right place and in the right way? Is there a Bethel in your life that you need to return to? Ask God for grace to respond to the lessons He is teaching you in this lesson.

God Reconfirms the Promises
Genesis 34–36

If Satan cannot destroy *Yahweh's* people, he will try to dilute their commitment to God. Genesis 34 records a tragic event—the rape of Jacob's daughter Dinah—and a dangerous proposition. The Canaanites of Shechem suggest intermarrying with Jacob's clan, which would have been catastrophic for God's purpose. Throughout their history, Israel struggled with God's command to keep themselves a distinctive people with a unified purpose—to know *Yahweh* and to make Him known. Jacob's sons reject the Shechemites' proposal in a sinful and excessive way. Still, God is faithful to the patriarch and his clan. *Yahweh* not only protects them, but also reaffirms His commitment to them in spite of their actions at Shechem. Jacob finally fulfills the vow he made two decades earlier at Bethel and determines that *Yahweh* will be his God forever.

The Defilement of Israel's Family

When Jacob departed from his family (Genesis 28), he promised to return to Bethel and fulfill his partially unfulfilled vow to God, which remains. Instead of honoring his promise, Jacob settles among the people of Shechem. Dinah, Jacob's daughter, goes out one day to visit the Gentile women of the land, and the local ruler's son *"saw her, he seized her and lay with her and humiliated her"* (34:2). Afterward, he decides that he wants to marry Dinah. Dinah's brothers hear of the rape and are furious. They decide to take matters into their own hands.

When Shechem's father, Hamor, begins to negotiate a marriage pact with Jacob, they plan to integrate Israel's family into their own tribe. The true threat to God's people emerges. For the remainder of the Old Testament, Israelites will struggle to maintain their unique identity. Had they accepted Hamor's proposal, Israel would have ceased to exist as a distinct people, erasing any clear public testimony to *Yahweh*. This problem will become so acute in a few years that God will have to move Israel into Egypt to preserve them as a people. Shechem appeals directly to Jacob and to his sons for the marriage. He is so smitten by Dinah that he is willing to pay anything to marry her.

Jacob's sons hatch a devious plan, basing their plot on the rite of circumcision. This distinctive mark is so important to them, that they cannot consider letting Dinah marry someone without it. Shechem will have to submit to the rite to marry their sister. Subtly, they extend the proposal to the entire city. Otherwise, Shechem will never see Dinah again. Hamor and Shechem immediately consent and call a meeting of Shechem's men to present the idea. Hamor points out the Israelites' prosperity and argues that the city will profit greatly from such an alliance. Shechem's men agree to the terms.

Jacob's sons wait until the men of Shechem are in pain to carry out their scheme. Simeon and Levi kill all the men of the city and recover Dinah. The other sons plunder Shechem, carrying off all its wealth, its flocks and herds, and the women and children. Their actions represent simple butchery born of resentment. Jacob reprimands Simeon and Levi and fears that their encampment will always be in danger.

Think about appropriate moral outrage. God hates sin and wants His people to stand against it. Dinah's brothers were morally right in being *"indignant and very angry"* (34:7) over the rape of their sister. However, their indignation turned quickly to sin as they chose deception, greed, and murder to wreak revenge on the entire city of Shechem for one man's despicable deed. How different the outcome would have been if the Lord had been consulted instead of ignored. God reserves vengeance for Himself: *"'Vengeance is Mine, I will repay,' says the Lord"* (Romans 12:19). That principle has not changed!

The Delight of Israel's Future

Jacob is sure his days are numbered because of his sons' rash actions.

God appears to him again and orders him to move south to Bethel, the scene of His original appearance to him—a gentle way of reminding him of his unfulfilled vow. Jacob prepares his family to go to Bethel and to cast aside their *"foreign gods"* (35:2). Newly sanctified by leaving their pagan associations at Shechem, God supernaturally protects them by sending terror of them on the neighboring towns. They arrive at Bethel without incident, where Jacob builds the promised altar, designating it *El Bethel, the God of Bethel*. At last Jacob is home, and God appears to him once again. *Yahweh* encourages the patriarch and again emphasizes his new name of *Israel*. *Yahweh* confirms every major promise that He has already made to Abraham and Isaac. Israel commemorates the occasion by building a stone pillar as a testimony to God's work in his life.

For unstated reasons, Jacob and his family move away from Bethel and head south toward Bethlehem. They do not go far before Rachel begins labor. She lives long enough to deliver her second son, but dies shortly after naming him *Ben-Oni, son of my sorrow*. Jacob renames him *Benjamin, son of my right hand*. Rachel is buried about 10 miles north of Bethlehem.

Again, Jacob is disappointed by one of his sons. Reuben, his firstborn, sleeps with Bilhah, Jacob's concubine. Reuben's actions will cost him dearly at the time of Jacob's death. This incident is an important event in the unfolding of Genesis. Simeon and Levi have already proven to be untrustworthy. Jacob will bypass these three sons when the time comes to issue his patriarchal blessing. Judah will inherit the ruler's scepter, finally to be placed in the hands of his great Descendant, the Lord Jesus Christ.

The Departure of Israel's Brother

The uneasy peace between Jacob and Esau will be reflected in years to come by conflicts between their descendants. Genesis 36 explains that these will arise because the Edomites become large and powerful rivals for territory. Esau built his family from Canaanite stock, with women who did not share his family's commitment to *Yahweh*, God of Israel. By marrying Canaanite wives, all traces of *Yahweh* worship fade from his family. His offspring would go to war with Jacob's from time to time, and the relations between the two nations would rarely be comfortable.

Personalize this lesson.

☑ There is no mention of God in chapter 34. Decisions that affect the history of lives, tribes, and nations are made without reference to God. Jacob the patriarch is Jacob the passive. He had seen God *"face to face"* (32:30), yet he failed to bring his great faith experience into his own home. When Jacob/Israel arrived in Canaan, he *"pitched his tents"* within sight of the city of Shechem and failed to provide moral leadership for his children in an immoral, violent environment. Our goal is to be in the world without being of the world. Jesus prayed for us that we would be able to successfully do that (John 17:15-19). What will you do to ensure that it will not be said of you that God was not mentioned in this chapter of your life?

Lesson 24

The Beginning of Israel's Journey to Egypt
Genesis 37–38

❖ **Genesis 37:1-11—The Chosen Son Elected**

1. How would you describe Joseph's relationship with his brothers?

   _____

   _____

2. What family dynamics influenced this relationship? (See also Genesis 29:30; 30:1.)

   _____

   _____

3. How does Jacob's gift to Joseph add additional fuel to his sons' hatred for their brother?

   _____

   _____

4. When Joseph recounts his dreams, how do his brothers and his father react?

   _____

   _____

5. According to verse 11, what sin is really at the root of Joseph's brothers' bitterness?

   _____

   _____

❖ Genesis 37:12-36—The Chosen Sibling Rejected

6. Why does Joseph travel to Shechem?

7. How might his family's previous experiences at this location have increased Jacob's concern for his sons?

8. How do Joseph's brothers react when they see him coming?

9. What does Reuben (the oldest brother) do to intervene?

10. Why does Judah suggest that they sell Joseph into slavery?

11. According to Genesis 42:21, how does Joseph react as he sits in the pit, listening to his brothers' cold-hearted conversation?

12. How do Jacob's sons deceive him regarding Joseph's disappearance?

13. Do you think the sons anticipated how deeply their father would mourn?

14. While his brothers are watching their grief-stricken father mourn the loss of his favorite son, what is happening to Joseph?

_____

_____

❖ Genesis 38—The Chosen Seed Protected

15. Which of Jacob's sons does Genesis 38 focus on?

_____

16. What happens to Judah's oldest son, and why?

_____

_____

17. What obligation then falls to the second son? (See Deuteronomy 25:5-6.)

_____

18. Why does the second son avoid his responsibility to his family and to his brother's widow?

_____

_____

19. What happens because he refuses to do his family's duty?

_____

_____

20. How and why does Judah also avoid fulfilling his responsibility to Tamar?

_____

_____

21. a. When it becomes obvious that Judah has reneged on his promise to her, what strategy does Tamar employ to reclaim her status in Judah's family?

_____

_____

    b.   When she discloses the success of her strategy, what effect does this have on Judah?

_____

❖ Genesis 37–38—The Sovereignty of God Displayed

22. a.   In Genesis 37, how do you see God's sovereignty in spite of human schemes? (See also Genesis 15:13-16; 50:15, 19-20.)

_____

_____

    b.   How is God's sovereignty also woven into the events of Genesis 38? (See also Matthew 1:1-16; Revelation 5:5.)

_____

_____

23. What have you learned from this lesson that encourages you to trust God in difficult circumstances or unexplainable tragedy?

_____

_____

Apply what you have learned. Clearly God had chosen Joseph. As a teenager, his dreams revealed that he was God's choice to lead the budding nation of Israel. Being dumped in a pit and then sold as a slave and carted off to Egypt certainly didn't feel to Joseph as if God were orchestrating the events of his life. But as the story unfolds we will see with certainty God's sovereign hand. God has also chosen those who believe (Ephesians 1:11-14). He may even place us in the pit for a time, like Joseph. Just as Joseph's dreams foretold his glorious future, so God's Word reveals ours! Pit dweller, read, study, and memorize verses such as Hebrews 10:23 and Romans 15:13. Your body may remain in the pit a while longer, but your spirit will soar.

The Beginning of Israel's Journey to Egypt
Genesis 37–38

The story opens with Jacob sowing seeds of discord among his sons by openly favoring Joseph, and the other sons coldly planning to kill the favored son. But then the brothers seize on an opportunity to sell him into slavery in Egypt, expecting that with that they have heard the last of him. Instead, Joseph prospers in Egypt and begins a rise to prominence through faithful service. Meanwhile, Israel teeters on the brink of losing its distinctive identity as *Yahweh's* people. God will have to bring them into Egypt for their own preservation; by this unusual means, *Yahweh* will show Himself faithful to His ancient promise to Abraham.

The Chosen Son Elected

Jacob, like Abraham and Isaac before him, is a man of faith in many respects, but at times he shows a conspicuous lack of wisdom. In his youth, his own parents' favoritism had brought heartache and division between him and Esau—yet it seems Jacob learned little from that experience. He openly favors Joseph. Meanwhile, youthful Joseph, lacking humility, aggravates the tension when he is sent to shepherd the flocks with his brothers. In some unspecified way, these brothers violate their father's instructions, and Joseph brings Jacob a negative report. Resentment boils over when Jacob makes Joseph a richly ornamented robe.

The Chosen Sibling Rejected

Joseph inflames a bad situation when he tells his family of his dream indicating that one day his brothers will be his servants. He has no control over the dream, but he should have chosen to keep it to himself. A second dream suggests that even his parents will be among his subjects.

Jacob sends the teenage Joseph to check on his brothers, who are at
Dothan. Because Joseph is wearing his colorful coat, his brothers spot
him when he is still far away. While he is coming, they plot the murder
of this brother they call *"the dreamer"* (37:19), and then quickly conceive
the lie they will tell their father.

Think about hatred. Joseph's brothers felt they
had ample reasons for hatred. However, the Bible is
very clear: *"You shall not hate your brother in your
heart"* (Leviticus 19:17). Once a person chooses to
hate, the door to other sins swings wide open. Violence
(Proverbs 29:10), dissension (Proverbs 10:12), and lies
(Proverbs 10:18) move in quickly, joined by malice and
envy (Titus 3:3). We, too, have our list of ways we've been
treated unfairly. If hatred is knocking at your heart's door,
don't answer it! Choose instead to *"love your enemies"*
(Luke 6:27) as God loves them. *"Your reward will be great,
and you will be sons of the Most High"* (Luke 6:35).

The brothers spring into action when Joseph arrives, stripping him of the
hated robe, the symbol of their father's favoritism. They deposit him in a
pit and callously sit down to enjoy a meal. Their lunch is interrupted by a
caravan from Gilead heading for Egypt. The caravan's approach suggests
a course of action: Why not sell Joseph rather than kill him? Their hands
will be "clean" and their pockets lined as well: *"For he is our brother, our
own flesh"* (37:27). For 20 shekels of silver, the brothers make Joseph an
unwilling member of the caravan.

Then they dip Joseph's infamous robe in goat's blood to simulate a
predator's attack. They take it to Jacob, saying, *"Please identify whether it is
your son's robe or not"* (37:32). Jacob is sure an animal has killed Joseph,
and is so consumed with grief that he can scarcely survive. Meanwhile, in
Egypt, Joseph is sold to Potiphar, Pharaoh's captain of the guard.

The Chosen Seed Protected

Chapter 38 provides a glimpse of the infant nation of Israel, which is
about to undergo a great upheaval. They will soon find themselves living
in Egypt, where they will be enslaved. What leads to this

drastic change? Israel is losing its identity as a distinct people. Judah marries a Canaanite woman, demonstrating a lack of spiritual depth. Their three sons—Er, Onan, and Shelah—live evil lives. Judah arranges a marriage for Er with a woman named Tamar. Because of his wickedness, God takes Er's life before he can father any children. In order to provide a line of succession, the brother-in-law of a childless widow was expected to marry her to produce children. Their children were legally the dead man's offspring and would inherit his property. Refusal to carry out this obligation was considered shameful. Yet that is precisely what Onan does. God regards his actions as particularly wicked and takes his life as a result. Tamar is once again a childless widow. Judah asks her to return to her father's home until Shelah, his third son, is of marriageable age. Judah has no intention of allowing the union; he fears Tamar may be bad luck to her husbands. Tamar honors Judah's request, but as years pass and Shelah is fully grown, she concludes that Judah has deceived her.

Later, Judah becomes a widower. Following a period of mourning, he goes to join his employees who are shearing the sheep in Timnah. When Tamar hears of this, she poses as a prostitute along the road and entices Judah to be a customer. She plans to become pregnant with Judah's child. She asks for a pledge to guarantee payment. Judah obliges, offering his staff and seal. However, when Judah sends the promised goat as payment, the *"shrine prostitute"* cannot be found. When Tamar is discovered to be pregnant, Judah determines to have her burned to death. She is on the way to her execution when she confronts Judah with the evidence of his own fornication. He reverses his order and announces that Tamar has proven to be more righteous than he. Jacob's story ends the same way it began, with twins struggling in the womb—this time in Tamar's womb. And again the younger, Perez, is the destined leader and ancestor of Israel's Messiah, Jesus (Matthew 1:3). This series of divine reversals proves again that *Yahweh* is the engineer of Israel's history.

Personalize this lesson.

☑ The 10th-commandment God gave on Mount Sinai was, *"You shall not covet"* (Exodus 20:17). Coveting may start with a normal, reasonable desire for something that another person possesses, but it becomes obsessive when you would sin to get it. You may say, "It is unfair that he got [fill in the blank] that I expected and deserved!" Jesus said, *"You have heard that it was said to those of old, 'You shall not murder; and whoever murders will be liable to judgment.' But I say to you that everyone who is angry with his brother will be liable to judgment'"* (Matthew 5:21-22). Coveting something that God has given to another person, but not you, can lead from anger to murderous rage, from deep longing to ugly sin. Even if you never "act out," but the feeling is there, Jesus has said it is wrong. Paul wrote to Timothy, *"godliness with contentment is great gain"* (1 Timothy 6:6). In what specific situation do you need to learn to be content with what God has given you? Will you confess your jealousy and ask God for what you need so that you can trade your jealousy and resentment for His peace?

Joseph Distinguishes Himself
Genesis 39–40

Memorize God's Word: Genesis 39:23b.

❖ Genesis 39:1-6a—Loyal in Duty

1. What evidence of God's presence and blessing in Joseph's life do you see in these verses?

   _____

   _____

   _____

2. In response to Joseph's God-given success, what responsibilities does Potiphar give him?

   _____

   _____

3. What conclusions about God can we draw from this passage? (See also Jeremiah 29:11.)

   _____

   _____

   _____

❖ Genesis 39:6b-10—Strong in Temptation

4. What new threat to Joseph surfaces in verses 7-10?

   _____

   _____

5. What new dangers does this pose for Joseph?

_____

_____

_____

6. a. Who is responsible for the temptation described in this passage? Does Joseph bear any of the blame?

_____

_____

   b. Who else do you think is at work behind the scenes in this situation? (See Genesis 4:7; 1 Peter 5:8.) What might his purpose be?

_____

_____

7. How is Joseph's fundamental view of sin critical to his ability to resist temptation? (See also 2 Samuel 12:7-10, 13; Psalm 51:1-4.)

_____

_____

8. From Genesis 39:6-10, how would you describe the difference between *temptation* and *sin*?

_____

_____

_____

❖ Genesis 39:11-20a—Steadfast in Obedience

9. While Joseph perseveres in his refusal to sin against God and his master, Potiphar's wife continues to try to entrap him. How would you describe her final attempt to seduce him?

_____

_____

_____

10. How is Joseph a good example of how to resist sin's temptations? (See also 1 Corinthians 6:18-20.)

11. What consequences does Joseph suffer because of his refusal to compromise?

12. Have you ever been unjustly penalized for refusing to compromise your principles? How did you respond?

❖ Genesis 39:20b–40:23—Faithful in Adversity

13. How does the Lord continue to bless Joseph, even in prison?

14. Why was Joseph so confident of his ability to interpret the cupbearer and baker's dreams?

15. Describe each man's dream and Joseph's interpretation.

Dream	Interpretation
Cupbearer:	
Baker:	

16. In return for interpreting the dream, what one favor does Joseph ask of the cupbearer?

   _____

   _____

17. Genesis 41:1 tells us that it was two years before the cupbearer remembered Joseph. If this had happened to you, how might you have responded?

   _____

   _____

18. Is there something specific that you have been waiting for God to change in your life?

   _____

   _____

19. When circumstances require you to wait, how can you use the time well? (See Psalm 37:3-8; Romans 5:1-5.)

   _____

   _____

Apply what you have learned. We live in an unfair world. Joseph was faithful to God and people in every way—morally pure, constantly serving and caring for others, and being obedient to authority—yet he was falsely accused and thrown into the dungeon. Justice was not done. Potiphar's wife deserved to be punished for her lust and her lying, yet the Bible is silent about any justice meted out on her. Unfair! How will we respond to such situations? We can count up the injustices, hold onto the grudges, and do our best to get even. Or we can respond with faith and integrity. The next time you are treated unfairly, be a Joseph. Remember, *"The LORD was with Joseph"* (39:21), and He is with you, too.

Joseph Distinguishes Himself
Genesis 39–40

Joseph's life portrays remarkable courage, stunning faithfulness, and, above all, his trust in divine supervision. With God's help, Joseph overcomes the incredible obstacles and becomes an example of how believers should act in the face of adversity. Jacob spent much of his life looking for ways to deceive and take advantage of others. Joseph, by contrast, is a man of conviction. He does not look for advantages, but only for ways to obey *Yahweh*. Stephen will later cite Joseph as an example of one who prefigures the life of Christ (Acts 7:9-18).

Loyal in Duty

Joseph begins his remarkable rise to Egyptian leadership as the property of Potiphar, *"an officer of Pharaoh, the captain of the guard"* (39:1)—a man of some importance. From the beginning, *Yahweh* is with Joseph in whatever he does. It becomes evident to Potiphar that his new slave's extraordinary gifts lead to great success. Despite being physically confined, Joseph is free to serve God faithfully. Potiphar makes the young man his attendant, and then promotes him to household manager. *Yahweh* grants His favor to Potiphar because of Joseph's presence.

Strong in Temptation

Joseph's attractive looks make him a target for the roving eyes of his master's wife. By this time, Joseph is in his mid-20s and has been in Egypt for about eight years. He must have longed for human affection. His master's wife boldly propositions him repeatedly, but Joseph refuses. Joseph does not assume an arrogant attitude, but carefully defends himself on the grounds that he would be betraying a man who has been unusually kind to him. Furthermore, such wicked actions would offend God. Potiphar's wife finds such reasoning irrelevant and continues to pursue him. Recognizing the danger, Joseph wisely chooses to minimize contact with her.

However, the inevitable crisis soon arrives. Joseph's duties again place him in a vulnerable spot; the staff is away, and Mrs. Potiphar seizes the opportunity. Grasping Joseph's clothes, she brazenly demands his presence in her bed, and he again refuses. He flees from the house, leaving his cloak behind. Angered, she uses the garment as evidence, accusing Joseph of being sexually aggressive. In her account to her husband, she twists the description of events, using a cleverly ambiguous phrase that clearly shifts the blame to Potiphar: *"The Hebrew servant, whom you have brought among us, came in to me to laugh at me"* (39:17).

Potiphar is enraged, perhaps because now he will again have to take charge of the household. Appearances must be honored, however, and Potiphar determines to punish his steward. Amazingly, Potiphar spares Joseph's life and has him thrown into prison.

Joseph's situation has gone from bad to worse, in spite of his righteous behavior. But instead of becoming bitter, Joseph bears up under the pain of unjust suffering, as Peter would later counsel Christians: *"For this is a gracious thing, when, mindful of God, one endures sorrows while suffering unjustly. For what credit is it if, when you sin and are beaten for it, you endure? But if when you do good and suffer for it you endure, this is a gracious thing in the sight of God"* (1 Peter 2:19-20). Joseph's behavior provides an example of how to be above reproach when temptation is unavoidable. Righteous behavior, however, may still produce painful results.

Faithful in Adversity

God's favor accompanies Joseph to prison, where the warden enlists him as an assistant. Rather than becoming despondent or bitter, Joseph shoulders his burdens and applies himself to the work. Even in such dark circumstances, Joseph experiences success from God's point of view. God will use Joseph's fine character to open doors of responsibility, all the way to the throne of Egypt.

 Think about virtue's rewards. We have no guarantee that virtue will be rewarded in this life. Our world value system is so warped that sometimes it seems character doesn't count. But this life is not all there is, and character does count with God. So we should all *"make it our aim to please Him. For we must all appear before the judgment seat of Christ, so that each one may receive what is due for what he has done in the body, whether good or evil"* (2 Corinthians 5:9-10). If only everyone believed that, what a difference it would make in our world. And though people of character may have to wait for their rewards, they have one reward right now—they can enjoy a clear conscience while they wait.

Two men, the king's cupbearer and baker, join Joseph in prison for unspecified offenses. A cupbearer was more than a menial servant. Cupbearers tasted the monarch's food and wine before each meal to ensure that they were not poisoned. Cupbearers were always in the king's presence, so eventually their role became political, that of trusted adviser. While confined in prison, the two officials each have a dream on the same night. Their dreams trouble them, so Joseph offers to place the matter before God, hoping to gain an interpretation for the two men.

The chief cupbearer recalls that his dream involved a vine that quickly budded, blossomed, and ripened into grapes. In the dream, the cupbearer filled Pharaoh's cup with juice from the grapes and placed the cup in the king's hand. Joseph states that within three days the cupbearer would be restored to Pharaoh's favor and to his former task. Joseph asks that, when elevated, the cupbearer remember him and do what he can to have him released.

The baker, listening to this interchange, is encouraged. However, Joseph explains that the baker's dream indicates that he will be executed and his body placed on a tree to feed the vultures. Both dreams are fulfilled three days later at the Pharaoh's birthday feast. The cupbearer is removed from prison and restored to his former position, and the baker is hanged. In his excitement at being reinstated, however, the chief cupbearer forgets Joseph's appeal, and the young man remains in prison.

Personalize this lesson.

☑ Repeatedly during his lifetime, Joseph had to make difficult adjustments. How could a man physically or emotionally adjust to so many dramatic changes? He was a man who had an amazing ability to trust God. He was a remarkably gifted man, but the key to his ability to adjust was his ability to trust. Life is made up of changes, and most of us don't really like change. Are you facing an adjustment right now that is very difficult for you? Think of Joseph and ask God to give you the faith to handle it with grace as he did. The answer for him was to trust God. The answer is the same for you. What are some ways to develop greater trust in God?

Recognition and Reunion
Genesis 41–42

Memorize God's Word: Genesis 41:52b.

❖ Genesis 41:1-40—God Troubles Pharaoh

1. a. How does the passage describe Pharaoh's dreams?

    _____

    _____

    b. Why did the dreams trouble him?

    _____

    _____

2. a. How is Joseph introduced into this situation?

    _____

    b. What can we learn about God from this?

    _____

    _____

3. What does Joseph tell Pharaoh his dreams mean?

    _____

    _____

4. After interpreting the dreams, what additional counsel does Joseph offer Pharaoh?

    _____

    _____

5. How does the king respond to Joseph's counsel?

_____

_____

_____

❖ Genesis 41:41-57—God Elevates Joseph

6. How long has it been since Joseph's brothers sold him into slavery? (Compare Genesis 37:2 with 41:46.)

_____

7. What new position will Joseph now have in Egypt?

_____

8. After establishing him in this new position of power, in what other ways does God continue to bless Joseph?

_____

_____

9. What is the significance of the names of Joseph's sons?

_____

_____

10. Have you ever had the experience of being fruitful *"in the land of* [your] *affliction"*? Please explain.

_____

_____

11. How widespread is the famine that Joseph foretold?

_____

_____

12. How has Joseph's God-given wisdom put Egypt in a unique position at this time?

_____

_____

❖ Genesis 42:1-38—Joseph's Brothers Come to Egypt

13. a.   Why have Joseph's brothers come to Egypt?

   _____

   b.   Why wasn't Benjamin with them?

   _____

   c.   What does this tell us about Jacob?

   _____

   _____

14. How would you describe Joseph's initial reunion with his brothers?

   _____

   _____

15. What do you think Joseph is trying to learn about his brothers by hiding his identity?

   _____

   _____

   _____

16. What strategy does he use to test them?

   _____

   _____

   _____

17. At the end of this first encounter with his brothers, what causes Joseph to turn aside and weep?

   _____

   _____

18. Why do you think he insists that Benjamin go back to Egypt?

   _____

   _____

19. What additional test do they encounter on the way home?

_____

_____

20. Whose hand do the brothers see in this alarming turn of events? Why do you think they have come to this conclusion?

_____

_____

21. How does Jacob respond when they tell him about their trip and Joseph's demands?

_____

_____

22. Can you share a time when God used adversity to change you?

_____

_____

_____

Apply what you have learned. Picture Joseph standing in front of Pharaoh, first interpreting the ruler's dreams and then advising him about how to deal with Egypt's next 14 years! Joseph gave God the credit repeatedly. What he didn't say is also significant. He didn't try to manipulate the situation. He didn't try to promote himself into the overseer's position. Showing humility and self-control, he simply stopped talking. How different he was from the boastful teen so many years before, sharing his dreams of glory. Can you think of a relationship or a situation in which God may be asking you to choose to exercise humility and self-control instead of "tooting your own horn"? Joseph was made prime minister of Egypt without having to recite a single one of his own qualifications! Trust God and allow Him to work on your behalf.

Recognition and Reunion
Genesis 41–42

Genesis 41–42 provides the remarkable account of how God elevates
Joseph to a position of great authority in Egypt and brings his guilty
brothers before him after more than 20 years. Instead of taking revenge,
Joseph wisely sets out to discover his siblings' spiritual condition. He
determines to seek their welfare in spite of their former treatment of
him. Throughout the whole process, he models a godly response to
injustice and anticipates the behavior of Israel's Redeemer.

God Troubles Pharaoh

The failure of Pharaoh's cupbearer to remember Joseph is a severe test
for the young man. For two full years, he waits in prison while nothing
happens. God's plan to end his confinement begins, like many events in
Genesis, with a dream. A confusing dream comes to Egypt's Pharaoh.
He sees seven well-fed cows emerge from the Nile and graze among its
reeds. Seven gaunt cows then emerge from the river and eat the fat cows.
The vision is so bizarre that the ruler awakens. Then he falls asleep and
dreams again. This time seven heads of withered grain consume seven
heads of full, healthy grain. The troubling picture again jars Pharaoh
from sleep. In the morning he begins to look for someone who can
decipher these dreams.

"All the magicians of Egypt and all its wise men" come before Pharaoh as
he seeks answers (41:8). Each admits his inability to interpret the king's
dream. Finally, however, the cupbearer recalls that two years before, a
"young Hebrew" accurately explained his own dream, predicting events
that *"turned out exactly as* [Joseph] *interpreted them"* (41:13, NIV).
When Joseph is summoned to the palace, he is quick to give God the
credit for any interpretation he may offer. Pharaoh presents the dreams

to Joseph, adding, *"I told it to the magicians, but there was no one who could explain it to me"* (41:24).

God Elevates Joseph

Joseph explains that the two dreams provide the same message: Egypt is headed for an era of great plenty to be followed by an equal period of severe famine. Joseph suggests that plans be made to cope with the impending catastrophe. He proposes that Pharaoh place a prudent person in charge of planning for the lean years. Pharaoh should tax the people 20 percent of their crops during the abundant years. They will hardly miss it because of the prosperity, and the accumulated supplies will help the nation survive the lean years. Joseph's advice, like his interpretation, makes sense to Pharaoh, who asks his officials, *"Can we find a man like this, in whom is the spirit of God?"* (41:38). Pharaoh acknowledges that the God Joseph claims to know has revealed the interpretation, as well as a wise strategy for the future.

Pharaoh elevates Joseph to the position of viceroy; Joseph will supervise the palace staff, and in all Egypt only Pharaoh will be more powerful. Pharaoh provides Joseph with the trappings of power, including his own signet ring used to seal important documents. He assigns a chariot for Joseph's use, and requires the nation to pay him homage.

Pharaoh also presents Joseph with an Egyptian wife named Asenath, and God gives Joseph two sons during the years of plenty. Their names suggest Joseph's recognition of God's kindness. The first he names *Manasseh*, from a Hebrew word that means *to forget*. The second son is named *Ephraim*, meaning *twice fruitful*. In his faithful commitment to God, Joseph recognizes that the years of trials have helped to form him into the man he now is, the savior of an entire civilization. When the years of famine arrive, the whole nation turns to him, and soon other nations are coming to Egypt as well. God is blessing the nations through Abraham's offspring.

Joseph's Brothers Come to Egypt

Among those who come to buy grain are Jacob's 10 oldest sons. The patriarch still plays favorites, keeping Benjamin home with him, assuming his youngest son is all he has left of Rachel. With his Egyptian clothing, foreign name, and prominent position, Joseph seems a stranger to his brothers and acts out the part. In this, Joseph is not being cruel or vindictive; he longs to know if his brothers have learned anything since they treated him so terribly. To test them, he accuses them of being spies. Their response reveals to him that Jacob and Benjamin are still alive. He puts them all in prison for three days, and then insists that they prove their claims by traveling to Canaan and returning with Benjamin. They will have to leave one brother behind as a guarantee that they will return. Not realizing Joseph can understand their language, the brothers talk openly with each other. They recognize God's justice in the situation because of their treatment of Joseph years before.

Think about the torment of guilt. Numbers 32:23 says, *"Be sure that your sin will find you out."* Jacob's 10 sons must have been nagged by guilt for years. The minute they encountered what they considered unfair treatment, they were convicted of their cruelty to their younger brother. Their words reveal that they feel they deserve the harsh treatment. It is horrible to have guilt troubling your soul. If you are carrying unresolved guilt, isn't it time to make it right? Apologize, ask for forgiveness, and repay what you owe. Remember, all sin is ultimately against God, so start with Him. This is the way to peace.

The brothers' discussion brings Joseph to tears, though he hides it from them. He selects Simeon to remain behind. He secretly returns the purchase price of their grain into each bag and sends them away, after providing food for their journey. The discovery of the money plunges the brothers into uncertainty. Arriving in Canaan, they report these events to Jacob, including Joseph's demand that Benjamin return with them to Egypt. Sadly, Jacob sees these events as part of a grand conspiracy to make his life sorrowful. He steadfastly refuses to allow Benjamin to go down to Egypt. For a while there is food; beyond that, the brothers wonder about the fate of their entire family.

Personalize this lesson.

☑ The apostle Paul wrote the principles Joseph lived out: *"Repay no one evil for evil, but give thought to do what is honorable in the sight of all. If possible, so far as it depends on you, live peaceably with all. Beloved, never avenge yourselves"* (Romans 12:17-19). Joseph could have easily avenged himself; however, he was a godly man who had obviously forgiven his brothers years before. His actions were designed to bring his family together again. His brothers needed to deal with the guilt they had kept hidden so long, and the family needed to be reunited so they could fulfill God's plan.

Have hurtful words or deeds driven a wedge between members of your family or between you and a friend? Could your negative attitude be interfering with some plan of God? Romans 12:21 says, *"Do not be overcome by evil, but overcome evil with good."* Go try to get it straightened out. Don't miss an opportunity to be a positive part of God's glorious plans!

The Testing of Joseph's Brothers
Genesis 43–44

❖ **Genesis 43:1-14—A Test for Responsibility**

1. Why has Jacob delayed sending his sons back to Egypt for more food? (See Genesis 42:33-34, 38.)

   _____

   _____

2. Who does he blame for the Egyptian ruler's (Joseph's) demands? Is this really their fault?

   _____

3. Which son volunteers to be responsible for Benjamin's safety? How does this contrast with his previous failure to honor family commitments? (See Genesis 38.)

   _____

   _____

4. Who does Jacob ultimately have to trust with his beloved Benjamin's life?

   _____

   _____

5. How is his statement of submission to God's will in 43:14 similar to Queen Esther's in Esther 4:16?

   _____

   _____

6. Have you ever found yourself in a critical situation in which you could do nothing except trust in God? How did you see God at work in that situation?

_____

_____

7. If you face an impossible situation, are you willing to entrust it to the one for whom nothing is impossible? What assurance of God's trustworthiness do the following verses give you?

a. Nahum 1:7 _____

_____

b. John 14:1 _____

_____

c. Philippians 4:6-7, 19 _____

_____

❖ Genesis 43:15-34—A Test for Jealousy

8. What is Joseph's first step when his brothers arrive in Egypt?

_____

_____

9. How do his brothers interpret his intentions?

_____

10. How does Joseph's steward reassure them and relieve their fears?

_____

_____

11. What questions does Joseph ask when they meet him there?

_____

_____

12. Why is this so emotional for Joseph? How does he react?

_____

13. a.   What test has Joseph prepared for his brothers when they join him for dinner?

_____

_____

   b.   Do you think the brothers passed the test? Why or why not?

_____

_____

14. How do you react when someone you work with or are close to receives special favor and you don't?

_____

_____

❖ Genesis 44:1-34—A Test for Loyalty

15. Joseph has prepared one last test for his brothers. From verses 1-13, how would you explain his strategy?

_____

_____

16. What does the test's outcome tell Joseph about his brothers?

_____

_____

17. a.   What does Judah offer to do on behalf of Benjamin?

_____

_____

   b.   Why is he willing to make this sacrifice?

_____

_____

18. NOTE: *Forgiveness* and *reconciliation* are not the same. We are commanded to forgive *"as the Lord has forgiven you"* (Colossians 3:13). But there are several steps to restoring a relationship fractured by injustice or injury. It's possible that someone may

refuse to reconcile. God's Word addresses this: *"If possible, so far as it depends on you, live peaceably with all"* (Romans 12:18). Here are the steps to reconciliation:

a. The hurt person must give up the desire for revenge, and trust God to judge justly.

b. Second, he or she must acknowledge both the wrong that was done, and name the wrongdoer. The guilty person listens, then responds by admitting his or her guilt.

c. The third step—reconciliation—depends on the guilty person's true repentance. When sin is confessed, acknowledged, and forgiven, reconciliation is possible.

Which step in this process was Joseph working through with these four tests? Which step(s) had he already taken?

_____

_____

Apply what you have learned. God had an agenda with Jacob's sons: They needed to become unified as the nation of Israel. One of the beautiful results of Joseph's tests of his brothers was their emerging loyalty to Benjamin and to their father. Did you notice 44:13? When the silver cup was found in Benjamin's sack, *"they tore their clothes, and every man loaded his donkey, and they returned to the city."* Nobody ran in the other direction to save his own skin, nor did they abandon their youngest brother. In fact, Judah begged to take Benjamin's place of punishment. They became their brother's keepers. In His high priestly prayer, Jesus asks the Father for believers, His body—the church—to *"become perfectly one"* (John 17:23). Let us be part of the answer to our Savior's prayer and reach out to fellow believers in loyalty and unity. In Christ, we, too, are our brothers' (and sisters') "keepers." Who needs your care or protection today?

The Testing of Joseph's Brothers
Genesis 43–44

Few Scripture passages can match the emotional tension of Genesis 43–44. Joseph's brothers are puzzled by the Egyptian viceroy's unusual knowledge of and interest in their affairs. Joseph's manipulation of events confuses them, but we can see the profound wisdom and affection that motivates these plans. Joseph's genuine love for his brothers cannot be expressed until he determines their character. If they come to Benjamin's defense, they will delight Joseph's heart.

Joseph Tests His Brothers for Jealousy

In God's providence, Joseph has risen to become Egypt's viceroy and is now in position to take vengeance for his brothers' cruel act of selling him into slavery 20 years before. He does not do so, because he is seeking God's interests. At his insistence, during their first trip, his brothers had left Simeon behind to guarantee Benjamin's return. Joseph wants to see what the brothers have learned in the preceding two decades.

Jacob has entered a state of denial. The famine is severe, and the area is completely dependent on Egypt for grain. Eventually, Jacob will have to send his sons there for more food, but he is unwilling to face this fact. Jacob seems to be content to allow Simeon to waste away in prison. Now he wants to ignore the reported demands of *"the man"* in Egypt (43:3). Judah forcefully reminds him of the viceroy's stern warning that Simeon's release and the purchase of additional food depends on their taking Benjamin to Egypt.

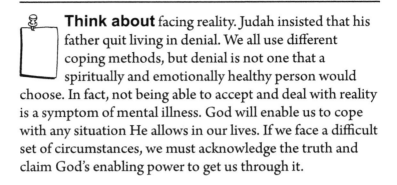

Think about facing reality. Judah insisted that his father quit living in denial. We all use different coping methods, but denial is not one that a spiritually and emotionally healthy person would choose. In fact, not being able to accept and deal with reality is a symptom of mental illness. God will enable us to cope with any situation He allows in our lives. If we face a difficult set of circumstances, we must acknowledge the truth and claim God's enabling power to get us through it.

The family's leadership is about to be passed to the next generation— provided by Judah, who guarantees Benjamin's safe return. Judah knows that failure to meet Joseph's conditions might well result in the deaths of all the siblings. Years before, Joseph's brothers had sold him, the favored son, into slavery. Now, the new favored son, Benjamin, is in their power, and they are committed to his welfare. They have passed the test of jealousy. Jacob at last bows to the inevitable and even proposes that they win the viceroy's favor by taking him gifts. In addition, the brothers are to take enough money to pay for the previous consignment of grain and to purchase a fresh shipment. They must take Benjamin, too, and trust in God Almighty.

The brothers again make the 300-mile trek into Egypt. Joseph allows them to come before him with Benjamin. Their reception includes a surprise: Joseph invites the 11 brothers to a feast at his home. Because Egyptians disdained foreigners, a meal at an official's residence would seem highly irregular. The brothers fear they will be falsely accused. The most horrifying prospect they can imagine is to be sold as slaves—the very fate to which they committed Joseph two decades before. At the arrival of this Egyptian leader who has the power of life and death over them, they present their gifts and again bow before him.

When Joseph sees Benjamin, he blesses him, but soon must retire to a private room to weep. The brothers still must face another important test, so Joseph washes his face, returns to the group, and orders the meal to be served. To confuse them further, he seats them in order of age from the eldest (Reuben) to the youngest (Benjamin). How could this Egyptian possess such knowledge? Although Joseph's servants bring delicacies from his table to all the brothers, Benjamin's servings are five times larger than anyone else's.

Joseph Tests His Brothers for Loyalty

Years before, these brothers had sold Joseph into slavery; now, he sets up
an opportunity for them to repeat that betrayal and sacrifice Benjamin
for their own best interest. He commands the stewards to place the
brothers' money in their grain sacks again, and he has a silver cup placed
in Benjamin's sack. Then, Joseph directs his steward to accost them
outside the city and accuse them of stealing his cup, waiting until the
very end to look in Benjamin's sack. Joseph wants to know if his brothers
will abandon Benjamin as they once abandoned him. But rather than
fleeing for their lives, they return to plead for Joseph's mercy, throwing
themselves to the ground before him. Judah steps forward as Benjamin's
advocate. He admits that though the brothers are innocent in this case,
they have guilt enough of their own. God's justice has finally caught up
with them. Benjamin's life is now in Joseph's hands.

Judah Pleads for His Brother's Release

In his defense speech, Judah retells the entire Joseph story. He realizes
the greatness of the man who will decide Benjamin's fate. He reminds
the viceroy that the brothers share a deep respect for their aged father.
The patriarch has already lost a beloved son, and now it appears that
he is about to lose another. His words show no trace of bitterness or
jealousy. Jacob's love of Rachel's sons was once a point of great distress
to these men; now they simply accept their father for who he is. They
have returned with Benjamin only out of absolute necessity. When they
were ordered to return, their father was heartbroken and insisted that
if anything should happen to Benjamin, his own life would be over; he
simply would not be able to survive the loss of the only remaining son of
his deceased favored wife.

Judah then proposes to take Benjamin's place as a guarantee of
Benjamin's safe return. Judah's love for Jacob emerges strongly in this
proposal. He would rather die himself than see his father so miserable.
Judah's offer to suffer so that his brother can go free is precisely the
climax of the drama that Joseph has been seeking. The brothers have
passed the loyalty test; there is no longer any reason for Joseph to
conceal his identity.

Personalize this lesson.

In chapter 44, Joseph gives his brothers the ultimate test. It will prove whether or not their hearts have been changed. They cannot bear to see their father hurt again. They obviously feel what is happening is divine retribution. These are the same men who callously enjoyed lunch while young Joseph pled for his life from the bottom of a cistern. Then they sent him off to Egypt, sold as a slave. Finally they dipped his coat of many colors in animal blood and unscrupulously took it to their father, apparently without the slightest concern about their father's feelings. Now their father's feelings are paramount in their thoughts. Never doubt that people can truly change—including you. If you have trusted Christ as your Savior, think back to your life before you trusted Him and list some changes you see in your life.

Joseph Reveals His Identity
Genesis 45–46

Memorize God's Word: Genesis 45:8a.

❖ Genesis 45:1-15—Joseph Reveals His Identity to His Brothers

1. Why does Joseph finally reveal his identity to his brothers?

2. How do they respond to his revelation, and why?

3. What thoughts must have flooded their minds at that moment?

4. What reason does Joseph use to reassure and extend forgiveness to these men who had treated him so callously?

5. a. How does faith in God's sovereignty and goodness change a person's perspective on suffering?

b.   How is such faith also an important factor in your ability to forgive those who have hurt you?

_____

_____

6.   How does Joseph demonstrate unconditional love and forgiveness to his brothers? Do they deserve it?

_____

_____

_____

7.   Based on the following passages, how has God demonstrated unconditional love and forgiveness to us?

a.   John 3:16 _____

_____

b.   Romans 5:8-9 _____

_____

_____

c.   Titus 3:4-5 _____

_____

❖ Genesis 45:16-28—Joseph Sends for His Father

8.   What does Pharaoh's reaction to the news of Joseph's reunion with his brothers tell us about his regard for Joseph?

_____

_____

9.   What does Joseph provide for his brothers' journey?

_____

_____

10. What parting instructions does Joseph have for them?

_____

_____

11. Considering Jacob's reaction in 45:25-28, what do you think it was like for Jacob to learn that his beloved son, whom he thought was dead, is alive?

_____

_____

12. Do you think Joseph's brothers disclosed what they had done to him? (See Genesis 49:22-23.)

_____

_____

❖ Genesis 46:1-4—Jacob Stops at Beersheba

13. Why does Jacob stop at Beersheba before he leaves for Egypt?

_____

_____

14. What barrier to Jacob's peace of mind may have remained? (See Genesis 26:2-3; 31:3; 35:1.)

_____

_____

15. a.   How does God reveal His will to Jacob that night?

_____

   b.   What message does He give Jacob at that time?

_____

_____

   c.   What specific promises does He make?

_____

_____

❖ Genesis 46:5-34—Israel's Journey to Egypt

16. How would you describe Jacob's reunion with Joseph?

_____

17. a. What location has Joseph chosen for his family's new home?

_____

    b. What is he counting on to ensure that Pharaoh will endorse this choice?

_____

_____

18. Why would it be important for this emerging nation to live apart from the Egyptians?

_____

_____

Apply what you have learned. Imagine being one of Joseph's brothers. Imagine the load of guilt you've carried for more than 20 years. Now imagine coming face to face with the brother you had so horribly wronged those many years before. Worse yet, imagine that this horribly wronged brother now holds your life in his hands. Contemplate the fear and self-loathing you might feel. "Thank God," you might say, "that I was not one of those brothers." But you are—we all are. Although Joseph was a real person who lived his own unique life, God arranged the circumstances of his life so that he would serve as one of the clearest examples ever of the Messiah—Jesus, the Brother each of us has so horribly wronged, the Brother who so graciously forgives us. Ultimately, every wrong—every sin— is against this "Brother." Will you allow Him to forgive you— and to forgive those who have wronged you? Who might you need to forgive?

Joseph Reveals His Identity
Genesis 45–46

It would be understandable if Joseph confronted his brothers harshly and rebuked them, but he does not. He has tested them and seen that, instead of abandoning Benjamin, they defended him. He has now set the stage for the dramatic revelation of his incredible secret. He will prove to be the savior of the brothers who have treated him so cruelly.

Joseph Reveals Himself to His Brothers

Joseph asks everyone but his brothers to leave and begins to weep so uncontrollably that his entire household hears him. He reveals his identity to his brothers and again asks about his father's welfare. Due in part to their own guilt, they are too stunned to speak. They had done everything except kill him. The one they cruelly rejected now stands before them as a sovereign ruler with the power of life and death over them. Who would ever imagine a story so unlikely?

The brothers back away, but Joseph calls them near so he can calm their fears as well as keep the Egyptians from hearing what he is about to say. (Joseph is no doubt speaking to them for the first time in Hebrew.) He is the brother they had sold into slavery. God has used their sin for good. Joseph's presence in Egypt and his unusual wisdom have worked together to save many lives. The famine that has already been so severe has five more years to run, but Egypt is ready. Heaven has used the unhappy events of 22 years ago to preserve Jacob's family.

Joseph asks his brothers to waste no time in bringing his father to Egypt. He asks them to explain to Jacob how God has given him a high position and vast authority in Egypt. Joseph does not insist that the brothers reveal their own guilt in the matter, although they do so eventually. He has already made plans to settle them in the region of Goshen, one of the most fertile areas of the Nile delta. Joseph goes to great lengths to show affection to the brothers who mistreated him.

Joseph Sends Messengers With Good News

The lives of the 11 brothers change instantly and radically. Before this day, they were subject to slavery and death; now they have access to vast wealth and resources. Before this, they were distant from the source of authority and power; now their family member is associated with royalty. Their changed circumstances picture those of Christian believers, who, upon conversion, find themselves in a totally new situation.

Because of his affection for Joseph, the Pharaoh extends Egypt's finest hospitality to his family. They will enjoy the best Egypt can provide. When the brothers bring this news to Jacob, his spirits are lifted, and he decides to make the long trip to Egypt. He must see Joseph before he dies. Perhaps at this point the brothers confess to their father their guilt in Joseph's disappearance. The brothers must have longed to be free of keeping this guilty secret.

Think about forgiving and forgetting. The silence of Moses, our author, about the men explaining to their father that Joseph was still alive reminds us that some things that happen in families are so private and personal that they are better left unshared. As for Jacob, it may be that he was able to see God's hand in the circumstances and to forgive his sons for their cruelty and deceit.

Jacob Moves to Egypt

Years before, God had warned Isaac not to go down to Egypt. Now Jacob is doing the very thing that God had warned his father against. This question is certainly on Jacob's mind as the caravan travels through Beersheba. This location had played an important role in the lives of Abraham and Isaac; Jacob builds an altar and worships there. God speaks to him in a vision and affirms that it is His plan for Jacob's family to move to Egypt, and his descendants will return at the proper time. The family of Israel that settles in Egypt is composed of 70 people. Four hundred years later almost 2 million descendants will emerge to travel to the Promised Land.

The climax of Jacob's trip occurs when Joseph rides out to meet him. The two enjoy a tender reunion after their 20-year separation. Before Joseph leaves them in Goshen, he advises that when Pharaoh asks about their occupation they should confirm that they are shepherds. Because *"every shepherd is an abomination to Egyptians"* (46:34), the Pharaoh will be happy to allow Israel's family to settle in Goshen. The territory is distant from any population center and is suitable for pastureland. By living apart from the Egyptians, the Israelites will be able to maintain their ethnic and spiritual identity, with few opportunities to worship pagan Egyptian deities.

Parallels Between the Lives of Joseph and Jesus Christ

Joseph's life anticipates Jesus' life in many ways. The New Testament stresses this point. There are probably more parallels showing Joseph as a "type" of Christ than any other man in the Old Testament: (1) both Jesus and Joseph were their fathers' long-awaited sons; (2) both held a special place in their fathers' hearts; (3) both were predicted to be preeminent; (4) both were sent to their brothers with a message, but were rejected; (5) both were sold for silver; (6) both were sent away to a distant place; (7) both patiently accepted undeserved sufferings; (8) both proved their purity and integrity when tempted; (9) both were wondrously delivered from their afflictions and exalted to the right hand of authority; (10) both acquired a bride with pagan connections (the bride of Christ is the church, which has been predominantly Gentile for the last 2,000 years); (11) Joseph became a servant in Potiphar's household. Jesus came to serve; (12) Joseph was imprisoned with two offenders; he pronounced blessing on one, but judgment on the other. Jesus was condemned with two offenders. He also pronounced blessing on one, but judgment on the other. Many more parallels exist, but these demonstrate God's direction in Joseph's experience.

Personalize this lesson.

☑ The similarities between Joseph and Jesus are so striking that it would take more faith to believe they are all just coincidental than it does to believe that God deliberately planned them. All Egypt, as well as Joseph's brothers, now honor, exalt, and bow down to this one they had rejected. In the same way, everyone will honor, exalt, and bow down to Jesus when He returns in glory. At the name of Jesus, every knee will bow and every tongue confess that Jesus Christ is Lord (Philippians 2:9-10). We now have the choice of acknowledging His lordship and submitting to Him voluntarily. When Jesus returns, everyone who has not believed will be forced to bow, but then be banned from His presence—forever. Who do you know who has not yet bowed in submission to Jesus? Think about the love, grace, and creativity Joseph used in helping his brothers accept the truth about who he was. Ask God to give you loving, gracious, and creative ways to help loved ones receive the truth about Jesus.

The Providence and Blessings of God
Genesis 47–48

❖ Genesis 47:1-12—Joseph Settles His Family

1. How does Joseph's strategy for Pharaoh's interview with his family reflect his God-given wisdom? (See also Genesis 46:31-34.)

   _____

   _____

2. What does he hope to accomplish? Is his plan successful?

   _____

   _____

3. What steps does Joseph take to protect his family's future well-being in Egypt?

   _____

   _____

4. What impresses you about Jacob's meeting with Pharaoh?

   _____

   _____

5. Select two or more seemingly unrelated events and circumstances of the previous 22 years of Joseph's life and explain how they demonstrate the truth of Romans 8:28.

   _____

   _____

   _____

6. What is one way in which you have seen Romans 8:28 demonstrated in your life?

_____

_____

_____

❖ Genesis 47:13-27—Joseph Saves the Egyptians

7. How do Joseph's planning and administrative skills save the Egyptians' lives?

_____

_____

8. How does he also build up the wealth and status of Pharaoh's government?

_____

_____

9. What is the people's attitude toward his policies?

_____

_____

10. How is the Israelites' status different from that of the rest of the population's? (See 47:11-12, 27.)

_____

_____

❖ Genesis 47:28–48:22—Jacob Blesses

11. How long does Jacob live after he is reunited with his son Joseph?

_____

12. What concerns Jacob as he approaches the end of his life?

_____

_____

13. In what ways does Jacob's last request of Joseph demonstrate his faith in God's promises? (See also Genesis 17:8; 28:13; 46:3-4.)

_____

_____

_____

14. In what practical ways can you demonstrate your faith in the following promises of God to you?

   a. Matthew 6:19-21 _____

   _____

   b. John 11:25-26 _____

   _____

   c. Philippians 4:6-7 _____

   _____

15. a. What terms of God's covenant with Abraham and his descendants does Jacob explain to Joseph (Genesis 48:3-4)?

   _____

   _____

   b. Why was it important for Joseph to understand the terms of the covenant?

   _____

   _____

16. What unexpected move does Jacob make when he blesses Joseph's sons?

_____

_____

17. Where in Genesis have we seen previous occurrences of the phenomenon that we see in 48:17-20? (See Genesis 17:18-21; 25:23.)

_____

_____

18. What can we learn about God from these recurrences? (See also 1 Samuel 16:7; Isaiah 55:8-9.)

_____

_____

19. What phrases does Jacob use (verses 15 and 16) to describe his relationship with God?

_____

_____

20. What phrases would you use to describe your relationship with God today? How has your understanding of God changed throughout the years of your walk with Him?

_____

_____

21. How can you daily demonstrate your faith in our Shepherd, wherever you are in life?

_____

_____

Apply what you have learned. In spite of his rocky start with God, Jacob is showing himself to be true patriarch material. In the waning years of his life, he is finally resting in the sure faith of his fathers. How much less his anxiety level would have been if he had arrived at this point sooner. Why do we fret so much? Jesus asked, *"Which of you by being anxious can add a single hour to his span of life?"* (Matthew 6:27). It might seem counterintuitive, but the key to leadership in God's realm is to relax—to work from a place of resting in faith in Him, rather than scheming to make things happen by our means. Jesus also said, *"Seek first the kingdom of God and His righteousness, and all these things* [provisions for physical needs] *will be added to you"* (Matthew 6:33). That's the key lesson all the patriarch leaders eventually learned. Will you ask God to help you to seek Him first?

The Providence and Blessings of God
Genesis 47–48

God will preserve Israel as a distinctive people by placing them in a part of Egypt where they will be free of Egyptian interference. Joseph encourages Pharaoh to grant them residence in the isolated area of Goshen. Their vocation as shepherds and keepers of livestock will enable them to live a quiet and peaceful life until Joseph has died and a new Pharaoh arises. During the famine, Joseph preserves the Egyptian population by providing food and seed grain from the abundant supply he has laid up. The Israelites prosper by God's grace. Jacob adopts Joseph's sons and offers a parting blessing upon them.

Joseph Settles His Family in Goshen

Joseph asks Pharaoh to confirm the decision he has made to settle his family in Goshen. He chooses five brothers to present before the king. When Pharaoh asks them to reveal their occupation, they explain that they are shepherds who intend to stay in Egypt only as long as the famine remains so terrible in Canaan. Their words convey several unstated key points: Because shepherds are repulsive to Egyptians, it is clear that the family has no social or political ambitions. Neither will they be likely to intermarry with Egyptian women. They request permission to settle in Goshen, which will place them away from Egypt's population centers. As Joseph expected, Pharaoh orders Joseph to settle his brothers there.

Joseph then introduces Jacob to Pharaoh. Instead of appearing as a subordinate, Jacob blesses Pharaoh. *Yahweh's* favor of Jacob gives him unapologetic status. The patriarch acknowledges that he has not achieved his fathers' age, and his life has known many trials.

Pharaoh not only gives the family permission to settle in Goshen, he gives them ownership of the land itself. This is in marked contrast to the Egyptian citizens, who soon will lose their property to the crown because of famine.

Joseph Saves the Egyptians' Lives

As each year of the famine passes, the Egyptians become more desperate. At first, they purchase food with cash. Soon Pharaoh possesses Egypt's entire money supply. When it comes time to plant next year's seed grain, the people pay for it by exchanging their livestock. The people trade all the animals to Pharaoh for seed and are completely desperate the following year. They ask Joseph for permission to be tenant farmers on their property that will now belong to Pharaoh. Joseph agrees to this proposal and gives the Egyptians what they need to survive in exchange for their property and their service. Now Pharaoh owns virtually everything in Egypt. The Egyptians consider Joseph's actions to be merciful. *"You have saved our lives,"* they say. The royal ownership of Egypt's land should be contrasted with the situation in Israel after the Exodus. God insisted that the land of Canaan be distributed by lot among Israel's families. Once the land was divided, it was to be held in perpetuity by individual families. Even so, they were to understand that the land of Canaan was a gift from their own Sovereign, *Yahweh*.

Jacob Blesses Joseph's Sons

The Israelites experience a significant population increase and acquire additional property in the area of Goshen. Jacob lives another 17 years. As he senses the end nearing, he sends for Joseph, who swears an oath to bury his father in Canaan in the cave of Machpelah, where his ancestors lie. Jacob is now ready to be reunited with his fathers. Soon the hour arrives, and Jacob rallies long enough to bless Joseph before he dies. Jacob plans to formally adopt Ephraim and Manasseh as his own. They will be honored as tribes of Israel. Reuben and Simeon have forfeited their rights to preference because of their violence and cruelty. The adoption will be Jacob's way of showing his delight in Joseph and his gratitude to him.

Jacob surprises his son by crossing his hands and formally recognizing Ephraim as the favored son of the pair. Again we see one of Genesis's recurring themes—a second son being favored over a first. Seth is favored over Cain, Isaac over Ishmael, and Jacob over Esau. Throughout the book, we see God make choices that violate the customs of the time and the parents' expectations. Sometimes it is difficult for parents to adjust to the prospect of the future unfolding in a manner contrary to their expectations. Part of Christian living involves allowing God to overrule our plans: *"Many are the plans in the mind of a man, but it is the purpose of the LORD that will stand"* (Proverbs 19:21). Joseph, who has seemed almost otherworldly at times in Genesis, struggles with Jacob's giving Ephraim the preeminence.

Think about unmet expectations. Joseph undoubtedly had plans for his sons. Manasseh, his firstborn, would hold the place of highest esteem, of course. And now Jacob has given the special blessing to Ephraim. Joseph's expectations are definitely not going to be met; it seems clear that his plan and God's plan differ dramatically. Have you ever found yourself in a similar position—unmet expectations and shattered dreams? Can you accept the fact that the change could even be God's plan? If the plan is different, accepting it may be difficult. It's hard not to be in control, isn't it? But we are not, God is.

Jacob, however, is speaking God's prophetic plans. He predicts that Ephraim and Manasseh will increase in numbers over the years. His words will come true dramatically in the years following the removal from Egypt. During the era of the divided kingdom, Ephraim will be the leading tribe of the northern kingdom. Joseph is comforted by the knowledge that both his sons will be productive in the years ahead. To sweeten the blessing still further, Jacob bequeaths to Joseph a piece of property. Jacob also predicts that Joseph will be taken back to the Promised Land. This would be after his death, when the departing Israelites disinterred Joseph from his honored grave and placed his bones in a cart. Once the land was conquered, Joseph was re-buried on property given to the tribe of his son Ephraim.

Personalize this lesson.

✓ Jacob saw his journey through this life as a pilgrimage. Perhaps it was because of the many problems he had that he never really felt that this world was his home. Hebrews 11 interprets his meaning well: They *"acknowledged that they were strangers and exiles on the earth. For people who speak thus make it clear that they are seeking a homeland. If they had been thinking of that land from which they had gone out, they would have had opportunity to return. But as it is, they desire a better country, that is, a heavenly one"* (Hebrews 11:13–16). Jacob was anticipating heaven.

When your life is comfortable and your lifestyle affluent and relatively problem-free, it's easy to settle down and think of this world as home. In reality, each of our lives is a pilgrimage. One dictionary definition of *pilgrimage* is *a holy expedition.* Our life here is temporary—a brief interlude to prepare us for eternity and determine where we will spend it. Our job is to put our faith in Christ and get on with the business of being conformed to His image. List some practical ways you can remind yourself that this world is not your ultimate home. Use this list to help you look forward to the home Jesus is preparing for you in heaven.

Lesson 30

The Death of Jacob
Genesis 49–50

Memorize God's Word: Genesis 50:20.

❖ Genesis 49:1-21—The Patriarchal Blessing of Ten of Jacob's Sons

1. What sin has disqualified Reuben from inheriting the birthright? (See Genesis 35:22; 1 Chronicles 5:1.)

    _____

2. In light of Genesis 34, why will God disperse the descendants of Simeon and Levi?

    _____

    _____

3. What future does Jacob foresee for Judah's descendants?

    _____

    _____

4. Who is the ultimate fulfillment of the prophecy in 49:10?

    _____

5. Read Revelation 5:1-5. What names reveal this eternal ruler's lineage?

    _____

    _____

    _____

❖ Genesis 49:22-28—The Blessing of Rachel's sons, Joseph and Benjamin

6. How does Jacob's blessing reveal his knowledge of all Joseph suffered and his awareness of God's sovereign care and protection throughout Joseph's life?

   _____

   _____

7. How would being certain of God's loving protection and care for your loved ones shape your attitude toward their journey through life?

   _____

   _____

8. What present and future blessings does God promise His children in the following verses?

   a. John 5:24 _____

   _____

   b. Romans 8:1 _____

   _____

   c. Hebrews 4:16 _____

   _____

   d. 1 John 3:1-2 _____

   _____

9. What must we do in order to be counted among God's children? (See John 1:12.)

   _____

   _____

10. Does God see you as His child? Why or why not? (See Romans 8:14-16; 1 John 5:10-12.)

    _____

    _____

❖ Genesis 49:29–50:14—Jacob's Death and Burial

11. Where does Jacob instruct his sons to bury him? How does this remind his sons that Egypt is not their permanent home?

_____

_____

12. How does Joseph's response to Jacob's death demonstrate his love and respect for his father?

_____

_____

13. Who accompanies Joseph and his brothers as they return to Canaan to bury their father? What does this reveal about the Egyptians' regard for Joseph?

_____

_____

❖ Genesis 50:15-26—The Sadness of Distrust

14. a. What assumptions do Joseph's brothers make after their father dies?

_____

_____

   b. What does this reveal about their view of Joseph?

_____

_____

15. What can we learn about Joseph from his response to his brothers' false assumptions?

_____

_____

16. As his own death approaches, how does Joseph affirm his faith in God's promises?

_____

_____

❖ Genesis 12–50—Lessons From the Patriarchs

17. As you reflect back on our lessons from the lives of the patriarchs, share one important spiritual principle you've learned from the life of each of these men.

   a.   Abraham (Genesis 12–24) _____

   _____

   b.   Isaac (Genesis 22–28) _____

   _____

   c.   Jacob (Genesis 25, 27–49) _____

   _____

   d.   Joseph (Genesis 37–50) _____

   _____

18. What effect has the study of the patriarchs had on your vision of God?

   _____

   _____

Apply what you have learned. The lives of the four patriarchs must be viewed through the lens of their relationships with God. Though each man had flaws and experienced trials of very different kinds, God brought them through better equipped to move ahead. And each had a personal, intimate encounter with God. God will also come to you if you seek Him wholeheartedly: *"'You will call upon Me and come and pray to Me, and I will hear you. You will seek Me and find Me when you seek Me with all your heart. I will be found by you,' declares the LORD"* (Jeremiah 29:12-14). Will you commit to seeking God more wholeheartedly so you can experience Him more richly?

The Death of Jacob
Genesis 49–50

These final two chapters of Genesis record the deaths of Jacob and Joseph and set the stage for the beginnings of a great nation. While Jacob seemed to make spiritual progress only through bitter experience, Joseph is another story. Even as a young man, he is convinced of the reality of Israel's God. By his faithfulness and trust in *Yahweh*, he saves millions of lives and reunites his family peacefully. In his death, he displays an undying hope in God's covenant commitment to himself and to his people.

The Patriarchal Blessing of Jacob's Older Sons

At the age of 147, Jacob calls his sons together to bless them and foretell the course of their lives. He summarizes their character and the effect it will have on future generations. He begins with Reuben, the firstborn. Reuben will not be chosen as patriarch because of his defective character, a direct consequence of his seduction of Bilhah.

Neither Simeon nor Levi, next in birth order, will take Reuben's place as the honored firstborn. Their lives have been marked by violence and cruelty, a reference to the brothers' role in the destruction of Shechem. They will be punished by being scattered throughout the rest of the nation. For the Levites, this dispersion will occur when they are made the priestly tribe and excluded from a single tribal area. The tribe of Simeon will own the southern portion of the Holy Land, but will mingle with the other tribes, and in time lose their distinctiveness.

Judah, by contrast, will become a leader among the tribes. His descendants will be powerful military leaders and will have the distinction of being the tribe from whom Messiah comes. This is partially fulfilled in the Davidic monarchy, but, ultimately, the prediction will be realized in Christ. Zebulun, Issachar, Gad, and Asher then receive their blessings.

Joseph and Benjamin's Blessings

Joseph is distinguished among the final six. He is likened to a fruitful vine. Though he leads an enormous Gentile empire, he is to remember that his father's blessings are far more important. To Joseph belongs the status of firstborn among the 12. Benjamin, though the youngest of the clan, is among the most aggressive. By the time of the book of Judges, the tribe of Benjamin will have gained a considerable reputation for bravery and skill in battle.

Jacob tells his sons that he is about to die, informing them that he must not be buried in Egypt. His body should be carried to Canaan, to the cave now occupied by his parents, grandparents, and Leah. As he finishes speaking, Jacob breathes his last. The patriarch departs from this world quickly, his struggles over.

Think about encouraging your family to expect great things from God. Jacob talked to his sons about the land they would one day possess, but it is clear that his emphasis was not on its material value but on its spiritual value. Addressing each son individually, he got their attention with insights into their character and future. He wanted to remind them of God's promises (though still unfulfilled) and God's faithfulness that he had experienced. Do you ever encourage your family to expect great things from God by telling them about His faithfulness to you? Do you tell them how God has worked in your life? And openly and unashamedly praise Him for His goodness in both your triumphs and your tragedies? Make it personal; that's what those around you will remember.

Jacob's Burial

Although all the sons were doubtless affected by Jacob's death, the writer of Genesis calls our attention in particular to the depth of Joseph's grief. His sorrow does not stop him from proceeding to honor his father's last request. He orders that his father be embalmed according to Egyptian custom, and the Egyptians mourn for his father for 70 days. At the end of the period, Joseph requests permission to accompany his father's body to Canaan, and the Pharaoh grants his request. The long trek becomes a state occasion, with many of Egypt's high officials accompanying the body. Joseph's 11 brothers make the trip, leaving their children in charge while they are away. The large entourage stops at the threshing floor of Atad, some miles northeast of the group's final destination, where they observe a formal weeklong period of mourning. The activity gives the area a new name, *Abel Mizraim: wailing of Egypt*. The group crosses the Jordan into Canaan, deposits Jacob's body in the cave of Machpelah, then returns to Egypt.

The Sadness of Distrust

Once back in Egypt, Joseph's brothers conclude that their lives are in danger. Now that Jacob is gone, they reason, Joseph will take his revenge on them. They are reluctant to face him, so they send a messenger with an urgent appeal. They say that Jacob left instructions before his death asking Joseph to forgive his erring brothers.

Joseph is crushed when he receives this communication. Do they know his heart so little that they think he is capable of treachery against them? When the brothers appear before him, they insist that they will be his slaves for life. Perhaps, they reason, Joseph will be content to enslave rather than to kill them. But Joseph knows the freedom of forgiveness and has no intention of doing them harm. Indeed, he has only their welfare in mind.

The family remains in Egypt for many generations. At 110, when Joseph is dying, he calls the brothers together and gives orders concerning his burial. He requires an oath from the family that whenever God calls them out of Egypt, they will not leave his bones behind. Four hundred years later, this promise will be honored when Moses brings Joseph's body out of Egypt during the Exodus (Exodus 13:19).

Personalize this lesson.

☑ The story of humanity began in the Garden of Eden, with two people in paradise. Their relationship with God and each other was unbroken. One sad day the tempter persuaded them to disobey God's known will by eating from the tree of the knowledge of good and evil rather than from the Tree of Life. Adam and Eve, no longer innocent, hid in the Garden. But God promised a Savior (Genesis 3:15), and from that point on, the Old Testament points forward to Him.

In the New Testament, we see this Savior, in another garden, praying, *"Not as I will but as You will. ... may Your will be done"* (Matthew 26:36-42). And in Romans 5:19 we learn that *"By the one man's* [Adam's] *disobedience the many were made sinners, so by the one man's* [Jesus'] *obedience the many will be made righteous."* Then, as the Bible closes, we see the relationship between God and people fully restored, and we also see *"the tree of life with its twelve kinds of fruit, yielding its fruit each month"* (Revelation 22:2). The Trees of Life—one on each side of the river that flows from God's throne—are no longer accompanied by the tree of the knowledge of good and evil. Evil will no longer be an option. This is the culmination of all history—eternal life with not so much as a hint of evil. God has called everyone out of the old garden and into the new one. Have you answered the call? With whom will you share this call?

Small Group Leader's Guide

While *Engaging God's Word* is great for personal study, it is generally even more effective and enjoyable when studied with others. Studying with others provides different perspectives and insights, care, prayer support, and fellowship that studying on your own does not. Depending on your personal circumstances, consider studying with your family or spouse, with a friend, in a Sunday school, with a small group at church, work, or in your neighborhood, or in a mentoring relationship.

In a traditional Community Bible Study class, your study would involve a proven four-step method: personal study, a small group discussion facilitated by a trained leader, a lecture covering the passage of Scripture, and a written commentary about the same passage. *Engaging God's Word* provides two of these four steps with the study questions and commentary. When you study with a group, you add another of these— the group discussion. And if you enjoy teaching, you could even provide a modified form of the fourth, the lecture, which in a small group setting might be better termed a wrap-up talk.

Here are some suggestions to help leaders facilitate a successful group study.

1. Decide how long you would like each group meeting to last. For a very basic study, without teaching, time for fellowship, or group prayer, plan on one hour. If you want to allow for fellowship before the meeting starts, add at least 15 minutes. If you plan to give a short teaching, add 15 or 20 minutes. If you also want time for group prayer, add another 10 or 15 minutes. Depending on the components you include for your group, each session will generally last between one and two hours.

2. Set a regular time and place to meet. Meeting in a church classroom or a conference room at work is fine. Meeting in a home is also a good option, and sometimes more relaxed and comfortable.

3. Publicize the study and/or personally invite people to join you.

4. Begin praying for those who have committed to come. Continue to pray for them individually throughout the course of the study.

5. Make sure everyone has his or her own book at least a week before you meet for the first time.

6. Encourage group members to read the first lesson and do the questions before they come to the group meeting.

7. Prepare your own lesson.

8. Prepare your wrap-up talk, if you plan to give one. Here is a simple process for developing a wrap-up talk:

   a. Divide the passage you are studying into two or three divisions. Jot down the verses for each division and describe the content of each with one complete sentence that answers the question, "What is the passage about?"

   b. Decide on the central idea of your wrap-up talk. The central idea is the life-changing principle found in the passage that you believe God wants to implant in the hearts and minds of your group. The central idea answers the question, "What does God want us to learn from this passage?"

   c. Provide one illustration that would make your central idea clear and meaningful to your group. This could be an illustration from your own life, or a story you've read or heard somewhere else.

   d. Suggest one application that would help your group put the central idea into practice.

   e. Choose an aim for your wrap-up talk. The aim answers the question, "What does God want us to do about it?" It encourages specific change in your group's lives, if they choose to respond to the central idea of the passage. Often it takes the form of a question you will ask your group: "Will you, will I choose to … ?"

9. Show up early to the study so you can arrange the room, set up the refreshments (if you are serving any), and welcome people as they arrive.

10. Whether your meeting includes a fellowship time or not, begin the discussion time promptly each week. People appreciate it when you respect their time. Transition into the discussion with prayer, inviting God to guide the discussion time and minister personally to each person present.

11. Model enthusiasm to the group. Let them know how excited you are about what you are learning—and your eagerness to hear what God is teaching them.

12. As you lead through the questions, encourage everyone to participate, but don't force anyone. If one or two people tend to dominate the discussion, encourage quieter ones to participate by saying something like, "Let's hear from someone who hasn't shared yet." Resist the urge to teach during discussion time. This time is for your group to share what they have been discovering.

13. Try to allow time after the questions have been discussed to talk about the "Apply what you have learned," "Think about" and "Personalize this lesson" sections. Encourage your group members in their efforts to partner with God in allowing Him to transform their lives.

14. Transition into the wrap-up talk, if you are doing one (see number 8).

15. Close in prayer. If you have structured your group to allow time for prayer, invite group members to pray for themselves and one another, especially focusing on the areas of growth they would like to see in their lives as a result of their study. If you have not allowed time for group prayer, you as leader can close this time.

16. Before your group finishes their final lesson, start praying and planning for what your next *Engaging God's Word* study will be.

About Community Bible Study

For almost 40 years Community Bible Study
has taught the Word of God through in-depth,
community-based Bible studies. With nearly 700
classes in the United States as well as classes in
more than 70 countries, Community Bible Study purposes to be an
"every-person's Bible study, available to all."

Classes for men, women, youth, children, and even babies, are all
designed to make members feel loved, cared for, and accepted—
regardless of age, ethnicity, socio-economic status, education, or
church membership. Because Bible study is most effective in one's heart
language, Community Bible Study curriculum has been translated into
more than 50 languages.

Community Bible Study makes every effort to stand in the center of the
mainstream of historic Christianity, concentrating on the essentials of
the Christian faith rather than denominational distinctives. Community
Bible Study respects different theological views, preferring to focus on
helping people to know God through His Word, grow deeper in their
relationships with Jesus, and be transformed into His likeness.

Community Bible Study's focus … is to glorify God by providing
in-depth Bible studies and curriculum in a Christ-centered, grace-filled,
and philosophically safe environment.

Community Bible Study's passion … is the transformation of
individuals, families, communities, and generations through the power
of God's Word, making disciples of the Lord Jesus Christ.

Community Bible Study's relationship with local churches … is one
of support and respect. Community Bible Study classes are composed of
people from many different churches; they are designed to complement
and not compete with the ministry of the local church. Recognizing that
the Lord has chosen the local church as His primary channel of ministry,
Community Bible Study encourages class members to belong to and
actively support their local churches and to be servants and leaders in
their congregations.

Do you want to experience lasting transformation in your life? Are you ready to go deeper in God's Word? There is probably a Community Bible Study near you! Find out by visiting www.findmyclass.org or scan the QR code on this page.

For more information:

Call   800-826-4181

Email   info@communitybiblestudy.org

Web   www.communitybiblestudy.org

Class   www.findmyclass.org

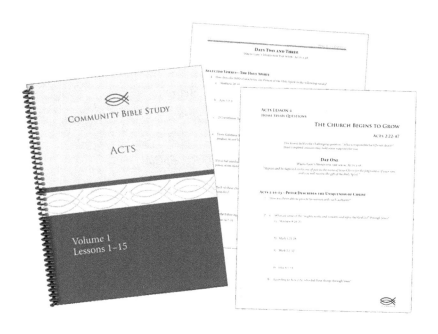

Where will your next Bible study adventure take you?

Engage Bible Studies help you discover the joy
and the richness of God's Word and apply it to your life.

Check out these titles for your next adventure:

Engaging God's Word: Deuteronomy

Engaging God's Word: Joshua & Judges

Engaging God's Word: Ruth & Esther

Engaging God's Word: Daniel

Engaging God's Word: Job

Engaging God's Word: Mark

Engaging God's Word: Luke

Engaging God's Word: Acts

Engaging God's Word: Romans

Engaging God's Word: Galatians

Engaging God's Word: Ephesians

Engaging God's Word: Philippians

Engaging God's Word: Colossians

Engaging God's Word: 1 & 2 Thessalonians

Engaging God's Word: Hebrews

Engaging God's Word: James

Engaging God's Word: 1 & 2 Peter

Engaging God's Word: Revelation

Available at Amazon.com and in fine bookstores.

Visit engagebiblestudies.com

CPSIA information can be obtained
at www.ICGtesting.com
Printed in the USA
LVHW020257301122
734320LV00012B/533